RAZING

Redemption of the Masculine Core

Razing Men

Redemption of the Masculine Core

Robert A. Revel

PHAEDRUS PUBLISHING
Healdsburg, CA

Published by

PHAEDRUS PUBLISHING
128 Powell Ave., Healdsburg CA 95448

Design by Caren Parnes, Enterprising Graphics
Editing by Rose Marie Cleese, Cleese Creative

ISBN 978-0-615-49143-1

Library of Congress Control Number: 2011931370

Printed in the United States of America

Not Shackled I, Nor Free

I am the wakeful, watchful one
The bearer of the hour
I am the noble dutiful knight
Guest in the House of Power
I am a madman like no other
Unleashed in mystery
I am choice engaged in servitude
Not shackled I, nor free.

—August 1983

This book is dedicated to Alice Simms

All poems quoted in *Razing Men* are by the author

PROLOGUE

It was the summer of 1999, in Paris, France. I was walking slowly across the gravel and dirt of an open-air courtyard, looking up at the encircling two-story balconies all around me. I was standing in an old armory, which had doubled as a military convalescent hospital during the Napoleonic Wars.

Something odd came over me. I stopped near the center of the armory's inner courtyard. The balconies seemed to groan as they cantilevered out over the grounds all around me, when in a flash I could feel a presence from above. Somehow I sensed there were these soldiers there, all gazing at the courtyard below, looking down at me.

Hundreds and hundreds of soldiers. They were all damaged men; arms and legs missing, torsos torn through, heads bandaged. Casualties of war. . . and somehow I felt this connection to them. And they knew me. More than knowing me, they had followed me into battle I was certain, fought at my command, gave of their bodies under my watch. It was all just a feeling, but it was unmistakable.

Then the most startling reverie of all—I could sense their complete and utter devotion to me.

Men who had given their bodies to war. Men who had forever lost precious parts of themselves under my leadership. How could they feel any kind of affection for me? And perhaps the strangest feeling of all was that I knew if I had asked them, they would have again, without hesitation, followed me into hell itself, and proudly given what was left of the life that remained to them.

I began to wonder. What had I asked of these hallowed souls when we had lived and fought together? Had my command over them been skillful? Had my leadership been true enough to be worthy of their incredible devotion? These men, it appeared, had crossed dimensions to give me their answer, and this book marks the first time I have spoken of it publicly.

There are few things as beautiful as deeply forged fraternal bonds. The heart of a man never forgets who was worthy of his love and allegiance. This book is an homage to the gathering of those honorable apparitions who did not want me to forget. I like to think that each page in it is a battle-worn soldier, who would follow me to hell and back.

WHAT'S IT ALL ABOUT?

Can you see the things that I see?
Can you feel the walls we call free?

— From *The River*

Who da' Man?

Writing a book about being a man seems on the surface to be a rather rote objective. Until you ask one simple question, "Who or what represents the true measure of a man"? Then things get interesting.

Think about it. By what standard today do we determine the true measure of a man? Where is it written? Where is it taught? Where is it even personified?

Being a man crosses all cultural and ethnic and religious boundaries. It is the common experience of nearly half of the world's population, and yet there is no collective, clear understanding of what it is to be a man. Why is that? How could such an essential thing be so profoundly overlooked in our current human experience? And more to the point, how are we suffering because of it?

Here in America, how to become a fully realized man is something they don't teach in schools, or in athletics, or on the job or even in the military. Learning to express the full masculine core is something that is really not taught anywhere in particular in our culture. That realization has become a driving factor of why I have chosen to write this book, because I do not believe that we have all quietly chosen to accept that there is nowhere to go to learn about authentic masculine expression in the culture. I allow that there are social efforts made to shape the character of our young men. There are perhaps private schools and other similar institutions of learning that emphasize certain character qualities or maybe detail some codes of ethical conduct. But the full scope of the masculine archetype runs far deeper than that. No boy will ever be able to unfold organically into the full measure of manhood by merely receiving lectures on character, or by having codified moral standards placed before him.

Scripting young men toward some program of managed behavior reminds me of the ways in which we direct the course of water with artificial concrete pathways and call them aqueducts. We call them aqueducts rather than rivers because aqueducts are simply lifeless conduits of managed water flow. Men who are merely processed with static doctrine become lifeless manufactured products of socially engineered behavior; they become the "aqueducts" of men. We need to find ways to nurture and foster boys in such a way that they will grow to become men who flow wild and life-giving just like natural rivers and streams. The question is how?

If learning how to be a man is passed on at all in any coherent form in the American social machine today, it is perhaps only from father to son, in the intimate bond where a boy simply absorbs his father's way of being in the world—for better or for worse.

But what is it that our sons are absorbing nowadays from their fathers? What kinds of transmission are they receiving? And what if the father is not in possession of true male wisdom himself? Indeed, in a broader sense we may ask, what if the entire culture of men as a whole has no consistent heritage of authentic masculine expression to draw upon? If the baton is not burning, how can we pass the torch?

I believe this is the condition we as men find ourselves in today. Since there has been no cultural or social context for learning how to be a man, there is in turn no available surplus of wise male elders whom youth can access who might otherwise guide the mass of neophyte males to a coherent potency. The blunt truth is that the male youth of America are mostly rudderless because, for the most part, our adult men are likewise lost.

As a result, particularly in America, we live in a culture that has vast numbers of developmentally stunted boy-men, giving rise to a peculiar lot of aging males who have no idea what action with implicit integrity is all about. The lack of a healthy cultural direction produces men who view life and their actions in it through a very narrow lens of mere personal perception. Such men will, time and time again, habitually take action based only on that limited perspective, often laying waste to or diminishing the environment around them.

Being an actualized man means acting only when that man's actions clearly benefit and contribute to life as a whole. The fundamental problem in this culture is that as men our actions typically reflect no allegiance to anything beyond a personal myopic worldview, and that viewpoint is simply too narrow to be of much coherent service to a broader culture or world.

As a rule, there is little wisdom in isolated perceptions that are fragmented from considerations of the whole. Men operating solely from personal agenda modalities in particular can become socially loose cannons, devastatingly dangerous and self-serving animals that heap a peculiarly vitriolic human violence upon the world. It is as if the masculine vision for wise, benevolent and graceful expression has suffered a curious miosis, and for centuries now our capacity for beauty has fallen well beneath our potential.

Today, male violence in America is epidemic. Our prisons are filled beyond capacity. Per capita, our women and children experience the highest instances of rape and molestation in the world. Urban America also has the highest numbers per capita of homicides. The sad truth is that today "road rage" is as much an American hallmark as baseball and apple pie. Yet it is not entirely fair or accurate to reduce the entire rank and file of American men into some dark man-beast, lumbering through the culture rabidly devouring victims at every turn. There are in fact more decent men out there then there are malevolent ones. It is unfortunately the sheer loudness of the malevolent men that gives the impression that a masculine brutishness has swept across the social landscape of America. It is the wake of destruction that the darker minority leaves behind that can shock the entire system into believing that we have a crisis of major proportion. But then the question arises, "How do the few continue to violate the many while being so outnumbered, as they obviously are?"

Perhaps most critically damaging to our social fabric is the inertia, the passivity of these so-called "decent" men who themselves stand by and allow the few gallons of toxic men to contaminate the entire pool of male social expression. These stand-by men commit a more insidious quality of passive violence through a smoldering self-omission, a suppressive unwillingness to do what must be done as men—

4

for like the malevolent violators, the passive stand-by males are their own form of the unrealized masculine.

The fact is that there are simply too many males who are simply not present in their core masculine power. We need these men to come home to the true masculine core that is their birthright. We need the passive majority of males to transform into authentic men to affect the shift in general male action that will help evolve the course of the human condition. There will always be a few men who go astray, but it is the sleeping majority of decent men who must wake up to their own potential and stand upright and true in the culture.

Reparation

What would happen to men if they are instead born into a social structure that gives them wise initiation and a strong counsel toward authentic manhood? What would it mean to us as men if our boyhood days could have been surrounded by role models of potent and beautifully realized men? What would have occurred in the lives of so many of today's unfulfilled men had a culture given them life-enriching options for expressing themselves?

This book holds as its premise that all men have the capacity, indeed the inherent design, for coherent and powerful masculine expression that is rooted in the wisdom of a natural benevolence and goodwill toward all. That masculine standard however requires proper activation, and just exactly how that may be accomplished is part of what this book will examine.

The first step toward realizing that vision, is to collectively put an end to the generations of masculine error that have placed us in this painful quagmire. We must accept that it is simply an error and not a human mandate or inevitability to flounder in aggression and violence. And we must take heart in knowing that error has remedy and that we may immediately embark on the acquisition of that cure for this and future generations.

It is obvious that we must do this for ourselves as men, and by extension for the survival of the species as a whole. But, even more urgently, we must do it now—immediately and without delay, for our women. For in the largest sense, it is our women: our mothers, our wives, our sisters and our daughters, who are agonizingly bearing the brunt of our whole-scale blindness to the true male core. Women deserve better. They deserve true men, real men—and they deserve it now, not someday.

The feminine, in fact, is the reason you are now holding this book. If you have a daughter or a wife or a mother you adore, this book was written to help you, ultimately, learn how to serve these women. This book exists in hopes that the majority of men out there are ripe enough to become worthy of the precious and radiant open hearts those women embody.

So I am challenging all of us as men to not only stop contributing to the unnecessary suffering on this planet, but also to transform into those true men who can provide for our women the safe and protective haven of an authentic masculine heart.

So here, men, is your invitation: for this moment, put down your hammer, set aside your pen, lay down your gun, turn off the computer, come down from your tractor, walk off the court or out of the factory, and turn to square off with the one thing you may have been sidestepping your whole life—yourself.

This initial act of stopping, and redirecting, is the first step toward being a fully coherent man. The act itself of stopping the momentum of error is a powerful medicine. That movement alone carries with it the tonic of true hope for a dream that is the birthright of your wives and daughters—a yearning for whole and beautiful men as husbands and fathers.

Let us now acquire the art of genuine masculine expression. It is time to begin living from our true masculine core and change the world.

2

Lost Boys

Consider the cost
Of the moment that is lost
To the kingdoms of men
And their ambitions again.

— From *We Fight*

The Myth of Maintenance-Free

Just "get in and go" is pretty much the creed of most American men. That is because men in general believe they are maintenance-free systems. Heterosexual men may routinely dismiss self-oversight, self-management and self-care as the peculiar domain of women and perhaps gay men. Rarely does a woman complain that her husband nurtures himself too much or overindulges in the self-help department.

Men want to contribute by doing things, building things, creating things, protecting things; the natural emphasis is to focus on things outside of themselves. They want to be of service in some way, and that service, they reason, is "out there" in life, not focused necessarily on their internal world.

However, the truth is that self-care, self-intimacy and self-knowledge are essential precursors to the capacity for caring for others. Men who are balanced, clear and self-aware will more readily contribute benevolent masculine action.

Unfortunately, our social framework fails to provide any structured context in which men are introduced to themselves intimately. Men are simply not taught the value and skill of self-intimacy. Men are not taught to cultivate within themselves the capacity to self-nurture, self-regulate and engage the world around them with what author Daniel Goleman has termed a functioning "emotional intelligence." The capacity of men to engage empathically or compassionately with those around them cannot unfold without their first establishing the cultivation of an awareness that is enriched with the foundation of self-intimacy.

As such, men launch into a life driven not from an intimate core sense of self-understanding and self-regulation, but instead from a distorted and unconscious functioning. They are also unrealized in their ability to establish a working understanding of their own self-limits. They may not be aware of or admit to the fact that they may not always be up to task. They may fail to acknowledge that they simply cannot perform in certain areas at certain times. Healthy awareness of one's own strengths, weaknesses and limitations, in combination with an ability to communicate and express them, is essential to core masculine development.

Men who do not find such balance within themselves will crave an artificially derived sense of potency. It is all but inevitable that these men will fall prey to the current cultural media hype about what a man is or ought to be, how he should conduct himself and what he needs to acquire to be "successful." Unrealized men who fall into this category of functioning will not intuitively understand how a man would properly care, serve and contribute to the culture and world around him. Indeed, as a man looks to and absorbs the cultural programming that saturates his life through mass media, he will by degree slowly become more deeply unconscious about the potentials of authentic male response within himself.

False Start

The "bill of goods" we are sold as young men about career and fulfillment in life is in fact at its worst intentionally deceptive and at its best significantly incomplete.

Too many times I have seen men come into my mediation office bewildered about why their marriage "went south" when all along they thought they were doing the right thing by being a "good provider." These men were genuinely stunned to hear that it is not enough to simply bring home the money and support the family financially.

It's not that the bulk of these men never cared to "show up" in other ways, they just never received any instruction on how to do it. As young men they were never taught the value of tenderness, empathy, compassion and playfulness when they were first learning to be men.

Wives turn to the husbands in my office and say, in effect, that they would rather have lived under a bridge with a man who knew, listened to and understood them all those years than have the big house and multiple cars and a man who isn't really there or emotionally available to them. That moment for a man at midlife can become an extraordinary wake-up call.

When boys physically grow into adulthood without the essential psychic foundation that would allow them to unfold into whole men, inside and out, they become ghosts (not spirits) in the world, and the culture absorbs them as such. The result, unfortunately, has become a mass of unripe men with no self-knowledge who blindly clamor about, intensely building their own house of cards that will one day, almost assuredly, collapse into itself. Wake-up calls to men in this predicament are inevitable; the choice to embrace an opportunity for change that is available to them through the present crisis is, however, optional.

The sad truth is that, as men, we have been sold a kind of fast-track-to-nowhere existence, and it is only a matter of time, perhaps within a few decades of living out the deception, until the truth will come home to roost. For most men it will come in the form of some kind of midlife breakdown where the old paradigm no longer fulfills and the current pressing realities become too painful to be avoided any longer.

Men will then rifle through the trusty old toolbox they have utilized throughout their lives to find the right tool to fix this problem. But the beauty of this new problem is that there will be no tool in that old box to handle what they are now facing.

It is at this awkward juncture that men may suddenly come to find that their lives have through the culture been steered toward an appalling non sequitur, and nothing seems to soothe the sting of it. The stark realization can shatter even the best-intentioned of men and send them careening into an interior abyss of disorientation that is invariably infused with a dreadful sense of powerlessness.

A feeling of betrayal in men toward a culture that has fooled and deceived them is not uncommon during the emergence of these painful realizations, but by the time these insights arrive it is so far along in the personal journey, that there is no going back to make it better. The passage is now clearly forward, however the direction and course of that path is far from clear.

Liar, Liar

We are loathe to admit that in a very fundamental sense our culture has failed us. We must concede that, on the whole, the social structure we all participate in is rooted neither in wisdom nor in a comprehensively benevolent action. In fact, the entire social matrix we find ourselves immersed in is intended to serve the sole interests of the few, mostly affluent men who designed and created this social system from the top down.

The architects and disseminators of social demagoguery watch as the masses continue to unconsciously drive the instrument of their own tyranny. The parasitic elite perpetuates itself with a majority of unconsciously unrealized men to serve a corrupt agenda day in and day out. Yet it is in our power to end this economic despotism. The self-entitled economic aristocracy that runs the soulless social order we live in could simply not succeed in a world where the majority of men had realized their true masculine core and refused to participate in the various regimes of social extortion we face today.

That is why the few who make the rules and set the tone and finance the propaganda in the culture are hoping that the mass of males will remain sheep and not convert to real men. A corrupt culture requires followers who do not question and do not challenge existing paradigms. Unrealized men have no core power, and when such men are exposed to cultural programming they invariably fall in line with the superficial indoctrination that the current power oligarchy culture emphasizes.

It is almost embarrassing to admit as men that the sense of noble and potent masculine service today has, for the most part, been supplanted by a blind patriotic-flavored allegiance to corporate propaganda that distracts us from the true impulse of core masculine expression and drains our organically gifted ferocity for benevolent action.

Throughout the avenues of social media we are exposed to propped-up, overblown caricatures of faux male potency that only dumb down and divide us as men. From a marketing standpoint, real men are useless commodities because, like Christ or Buddha, they will never be products of, or conform to, flawed socio-cultural agendas. The authentic masculine core is too alive, too radical and too authentic to capture and package.

The day that the scales tip in favor of a majority of men in their true masculine core is the day that the tide will begin to change for the entire human race.

We are raised inside a social machine that is designed to spit out sheep instead of men. Until we have enough true core change of masculine expression in the culture that can shift the tide, we will continue to have a society that produces propaganda about faux male potency rather than education about true male power. We will have allusions to certain socially vogue character traits, but no wisdom regarding the essential character of the true masculine core. We will have social indoctrination of boys and men into "power-over" strategies to achieve supposed success in competitive market spheres, but no initiation into the deep heart of authentic masculine activation. Without the fundamental humility of an engaged masculine heart, men will continue to celebrate self-aggrandizing and fail to cultivate the essential self-intimacy that allows them to move with tenderness and true power in the world.

We need real men. What is required is an evolved model of masculine standard that will pull us as a culture out of the role-playing caricatures that we have come to accept as tolerable male expression. At this point in our evolution, the time is ripe for change.

Lost Male Types

When a man can be reduced to a predictable pattern of behavior, he is more a caricature than he is a man. Many lost men in American culture can be put into four categories that I refer to as *Believers*, *Deceivers*, *Relievers* and *Conceivers*. Some men who are not in their true masculine core will compensate for the deficit by utilizing one of the above coping strategies. As we review these composites of masculine distortion profiled below, it will be hard not to feel sad for our women. It is altogether unnecessary that any woman must be forced to choose mostly from a pool of unbalanced men. It is in fact my hope that one day soon women will have a healthy pool of men to select from that allows them to discriminate to a higher standard of masculine embodiment.

Believers

Believers are a simple and predictable persona of static programming. Since they have very little sense of a self-core, they require somebody, or something, to tell them what to think, how to feel or not feel, and how to act. The investment in their belief systems can be extreme and dangerously inflexible. Men such as these often become violently intolerant to any other perspectives.

Religious orientation, class/social doctrines, political affiliations and ethnic affinities all conspire at times to indoctrinate believers into their particular subgroup paradigm and solicit for the allegiance of believer men to follow.

The renowned social scientist B.F. Skinner once proclaimed, "Give me the specifications, and I'll give you the man." Engineering human personality and belief through indoctrination has been a key function of many totalitarian regimes bringing great damage throughout our brief history as humans.

Believer men are foot soldiers who are essential to the success of totalitarian regimes. Without such sheep there simply could be no tyranny, no one to toe the party line. Because believers currently make up the majority of the human consciousness paradigm, we continue to suffer under the plague of social demagoguery that utilizes believer mentalities to serve its selfish ends.

Believers find affirmation in numbers. But group thinking is often vulnerable to corruption and has always lived under the weight of a peculiar distortion throughout history. Men who have successfully deconstructed their own personal subjective paradigm become free from the tyranny of their own personal conceptual framework and will by extension then be free from the deep influence of the dangerous box of group-thinking.

To be a man is to be free. No man who acts unconsciously under the direction of another's authority or out of some blind allegiance to static doctrine can be said to be free. To have real men in our culture, we must have free-thinking souls who respond from the authority of the fluid and intuitive heart. Until then, we labor under and are servants of the tyranny du jour.

Deceivers

Deceivers are game players, plain and simple. They are knowingly working the system of human error maliciously for their own personal gain. These men are renegade self-servers, and they degrade the world they live in just like cancer cells devour the body that hosts them. Consciously unconscious, these men know the damage they do, and do it anyway just to enhance their own personal position.

Deceivers must build their world of deception on a colossal foundation of denial, and as such eventually come to believe their own lies. The error of their extreme disillusionment will ultimately destroy them if left unchecked, but not usually before they have wrought significant damage to those around them.

Deceivers as a group have produced some of the most damaging male character profiles in history. Adolph Hitler, Jim Jones and Charles Manson are some examples of deceivers in the extreme. These men lie, manipulate and misrepresent, practicing their strategy of deception on all who will trust them.

Relievers

Relievers are escape artists. They seek whatever means possible to numb themselves to the realities of life. They tend to subject the body to some kind of drug or chemical so as to affect a physiological response that either mutes or distracts the senses away from their organically perceptive states.

Addicts are classic relievers running from themselves and the full impact of what their conscious experience invites them to feel. Some men use external chemicals, and some stimulate the ones in their own bodies, such as adrenaline and endorphins, to feel "high" and escape. Relievers tend to be sensitive by nature, and the impulse to "relieve" comes from a need to shut out the life they are so adept at feeling.

Reliever men are not just boys who were never taught to grow up, but actually choose to remain boy-like instead of becoming men. Playing is a creed that they have come to justify as harmless and irreverently appropriate to their disengaged lives. I have heard many women call these types of men "Peter Pans" because they never choose to assume the full mantle of manhood responsibilities. While often charming in nature, they manifest a stark deficit in their capacity to embody a full accountability for the things that a masculine emphasis is designed to embrace. For women not paying attention to the "red flags" these boy-men proudly display, this kind of male charmer can amount to a disappointing "bait and switch," stimulating upfront but no content in the main.

These kinds of men typically indulge in sophomoric activities like sports, partying, substance abuse or other recreational activities usually associated with the follies of adolescent expression. Such men not only squander precious time with these activities, but they also waste precious resources, often forsaking the mature domains of family, healthy adult relationships and meaningful culture participation for a life of relative frivolity.

Conceivers

Conceivers are men who create families or other social structures as a means of control. Creating an isolated family unit so as to finally have something that they can have control over is one strategy conceivers use to cope with the sense of powerlessness they feel inside. Controlling a wife and children while moving impotently through the world is the sad profile of this ilk of men.

Conceivers tend to live vicariously through their offspring. These hollow men project all their unrealized emptiness onto the youthful vitality of their children and suffocate them with their blanket of broken dreams, prodding children to fulfill what their father could not.

Conceivers are also particularly parasitic of the feminine radiance. Through the relative stability of a marriage and family structure, they deplete the feminine core of their wives because they have failed to arrive first at their own masculine core before coupling with the feminine. The broken pathologies of such husbands and fathers will over time wear down the vitality and abundance of the women they marry and use as comfort and support over a lifetime.

Conceiver men may also create businesses that they lord over like a mafia don, subjugating their subordinates to a tyrannical and/or exploitive work environment. Like the father in an isolated family structure, a business can serve as an imagined island of power that may bolster the conceiver's sense of self-meaning and efficacy when there is a lack of a true male core at work inside the man.

Conceivers create isolated structures that they can control and rule. Outside of these structures these men are often perceived of as shy or mild-mannered. The tragic effort at establishing control to feel safe, potent and secure is a largely unconscious behavior in such men.

The Large Perspective

No athletic coach worth his salt ever walked into a fresh season and approached his assembled team to say, "All right boys, we are doing enough already. Last season wasn't a winning one, but there's no need to focus on what went wrong—that's just negativity. If we just cut ourselves some slack and realize nobody is perfect, I'm sure things will get better for us."

If we as men want to change, improve and triumph in our desire to become liberated men and authentically masculine role models, we are going to have to pull out all the stops and quit handling masculine flaws with kid gloves. If this book's examination of men at times reads in tone more like Vince Lombardi then it does Mr. Rogers, it is because I know that what got us "here" won't get us "there." I know men, and I know that gentle suggestions rarely register with them.

As critical and as blunt as I may be at times about men, make no mistake that this book is an effort to redeem and not to indict the masculine archetype. It is by necessity that we must, with constructive criticism, call out the shadow side of the masculine and expose it for what it really is. Not all men are hopeless or even intentionally lost. Most men, I believe, are damn decent human beings, and a few men I have met in my life are truly magnificent examples of coherent masculine expression. In fact it is the incredibly beautiful potential of the masculine archetype that drives the vision within these pages.

So while we may examine the body of a suffering masculine culture, the effort is not meant to promote male cynicism or a general despondency. It is a movement to gain clarity and expose masculine error so that we may begin to affect reparation for a new and healthy generation of masculine unfolding. The "end of suffering" for our purposes does not mean the end of the natural pains and strife that come with the act of being in a physical body on this planet. The end of suffering means the end of the personal resistances that rail against naturally occurring organic life challenges, a resistance that ultimately breeds the tension we call suffering and keeps us groping in the dark about matters of real import. The affliction of resistance to what is happening to us turns out to be purely optional. The direct experience of pain may be inevitable in life, but the quality of our response to it is, however, largely a matter of our choosing. These choices become the very markers of whether or not we end up expressing a coherent or a distorted masculine persona.

SINS OF THE FATHER

I'm walking in the rain
Each drop like a tear of pain
Strung in the saddest chain
Binding me to those years long ago.

— From *Years Long Ago*

Original Sin

The bulk of human suffering is the history of the masculine archetype gone horribly awry. Fix the error of the masculine and you affect significant reparation of the entire human condition. This is no overstatement, and it is about time for a due accountability with regard to the subject. We masculine actors are those who started the existing cycle of violence, and so it is our responsibility now to initiate the end of it.

Men are the bearers of the "original sin" in this dance of pain and, as men, need to end it. Redemption for men is participation in the healing of the folly and error of our gender and reclaiming the true masculine core that was and is our birthright.

For too long now our cultural and social systems have either danced around the subject of masculine accountability or marginalized those who attempt to highlight it, calling them male-bashers, or as the scholars like to call it, an instance of "misandry" (i.e., hatred of men).

If a woman points out the obvious male error in the culture at large, she may be vilified as a man-hater or perhaps a ball-busting feminist. If a man points out the false hyper-masculine condition with a call to integrity and accountability, he may be summarily blacklisted as a male traitor, or perhaps even condemned as Jesus was, if he is a really serious threat to the prevalent male power paradigms.

There is a clear distinction in my mind between an indulging in misandry and the act of pointing to a necessary masculine accountability. Certainly women have come to participate in this culture of violence as well, even if only in a desperate or passive way. Most women would be the first to admit that they have, in their own way as a gender polarity, contributed to the general error found today in the human condition. There is no doubt that the dilemma within the human condition is a shared responsibility of both men and women, however we must give credence to critical differentiations between the relative social positioning of men and women before we approach solution. There is a clear masculine hegemony that tips the masculine/feminine balance toward an inequitable influence of male control within the social structures of humans.

Women historically hold a curiously subverted position within the species. I would liken the quality of it to the German soldier in World War II. We may assign an accountability for his part in the malevolent agenda of the Third Reich, but his relative access, influence and ability to change the Nazi power paradigm within which he was immersed as an individual was negligible. Nazi power was controlled and directed specifically by Adolph Hitler and his immediate staff of field marshals and generals. For women, the male-assigned social station they occupy mirrors that of the German military foot soldier in WWII, while men in the culture mirror the position of the leadership of the Third Reich.

For women individually it is difficult to affect change as a single point of influence because the social structures of men do not honor or value the import of feminine influence. Certainly a general, en masse grassroots revolt with resolute solidarity among all women would bring about a climate for leveraged change, but barring that, it is difficult to imagine an opportunity where women are granted the authority by men to affect the current crisis of violence within the human condition. Ultimately for women though, the journey and responsibility of their participation in it is theirs to decipher.

I feel more comfortable speaking from my own direct experience of being a man—and it is different for men. Men have created sanctioned social positions and self-endorsed authority. In spite of this however, the core masculine redemption of a handful of authentic leaders might, by example, effectively "tonify" the general masculine body of men worldwide and bring about a potential for constructive evolution of the masculine core. The current imbalance is not irredeemable.

Approaching the Problem

When it comes to the typical brands of formal masculine examination, I feel much time has been wasted on arguing about whether we as human beings are suffering under a "patriarchal" culture or not, or whether or not men have themselves been victimized by the social structures we inhabit. We would be much better served to ultimately abandon such designations as "patriarchal" and focus on the fact that what we are dealing with here is a culture dominated by men whose masculine expression is incoherent. The actual problem with men has nothing to do with whether or not men have social authority; the root problem is that the prevalent masculine embodiment has been stripped of the appropriate feminine integration that would otherwise give it coherency as an archetypal expression. As a result, the general male capacity to wield any authority at all in healthy ways has been truncated.

It is predictable perhaps that most of the legitimate approaches endorsed by social media to the masculine crisis tend to be those put forth by scholars. It is as if the study of masculine error were somehow the domain of the credentialed products of academia— all appropriate, of course, if that process ever yielded results that had significant cultural traction. But where or when have any relevant data from scholarly analysis contributed to the growth of actual masculine expression in the culture?

Scholarly review of the masculine dilemma often presents as a showy pageantry of clever concept engineering, producing little more than a labored intellectual treatise on social theory that often fails to strike the gut of a man. Many of the books I have read over the years on the subject end up feeling to me as if the hands doing the writing have never themselves been bloody enough with the problem.

Analysis is a healthy tool, and research is essential. We need to know the context of the problem, no doubt, and certainly we need to understand the error itself. But we cannot afford to depend only on well-articulated theories drawn solely from the nation's scholarly alumni. We need men with calloused hands who have come down from our culture's ivory tower of academic judgment and taken the real hits that forge men's souls. We need men who themselves have slogged doggedly through the trenches of the human condition, and not just reviewed it cerebrally from the detached perspectives of the intellect's creaky watchtower.

Waiting for sterile answers about men from detached intellectuals is, in fact, a dilemma that has kept authentic masculine reform at bay for far too long. The time is at hand now for masculine leaders and teachers to step forward and be the kinds of coaches who have played the game. It is a time for men who have actually embodied the integrated masculine to demonstrate living that authentic male expression publicly, be they scholars or prison inmates. This is the heart of the new order of masculine instruction that will bring about the reformation in male expression that is so sorely needed in the world today.

The Missing "Ink" of the Feminine

Women have the capacity to gestate, give birth and nurse human life. It cannot be summarily dismissed that women's somatically inherited expressions of menses and their potential for pregnancy and child-bearing shape their perception of life and the experience of living it. The powerful rhythmic forces that drive their monthly cycles and the mysteriously humbling experience of having a fetus growing to term inside their bodies give women a grounded sense of interconnectivity, humility and a wonder that among other things allows for the fact that they cannot control everything.

It may be argued that if men had a similar physiological experience in this world, where they too felt intimately and directly the inexplicable connection they have to the ineffable mysteries of life,

27

then perhaps they too would bear the mark of the tender and humble graces of the feminine archetype and be less prone to exploit whole cross sections of life.

Many ancient tribal cultures at least held the mark of the feminine within their traditional tapestry. They provided their men with ritual activity that gave them initiation into the qualities and understandings that women learn quite naturally through their bodies. But the feminine marker from those times and those cultures has for most of modern man been rendered defunct or at least reduced to a narcotic irrelevance by a rapidly growing worldwide indoctrination into cultureless consumerism.

It all begs the question that if there had been a general balance of polarity expression within the human condition, where the feminine archetype had influenced and contributed equally to the outcome of human history, how much different would that history have looked? How much different would our culture and social structures look today?

But it has been unbalanced men who instead have driven the tone, quality and bulk of content within the human condition from the seat of "power-over" systems that men themselves created—systems that, along with admittedly amazing achievements, have also wrought endless waves of devastation and destruction throughout human history.

To this day our daughters, our wives, our sisters and our mothers are being driven from the core of themselves and their natures by the unconscious and insensitive actions of the men closest to them. It is not necessarily that these men are malevolent by nature, but that these men represent and embody the flawed culture and by extension are reflecting a peculiar violence in relationship.

Young Guns

It is worth mentioning that the human experiment is a rather new phenomenon. With perhaps a mere 200,000 years of the human (Homo sapiens) species being on the scene, compared to the roughly 180-million-year run of the creatures that dominated the dinosaur era, we aren't even toddlers yet in geological time. The evolution of our hominid consciousness is still in its very young and budding stages.

Our relative immaturity of consciousness as a species, matched with our incredible capacity for conceptualization, linear thought, reasoning, logic and abstraction, makes for a dangerous and often lethal combination. Like toddlers playing with explosives, we are at present a very dangerous breed.

Our newness as a thinking species may have made us more prone to error in our expression than few have ever stopped to consider. The exploration of consciousness itself through the instrument of the human mind is perhaps just now emerging out of its freshman stages. This may help to explain our recent fumbling course through human history.

If so, what human mechanism was it in particular that gave rise to the peculiarly masculine error that has most greatly perpetrated the history of violence within our species? In other words, what is this purely masculine error exactly and how did it come to be? To answer this question, a little history is in order.

Square One

It is an anthropological maxim that we survive because we are social creatures. Like most other primates, we have always run in packs, clans and similar social groupings. The insightful statement that "a lone baboon is a dead baboon" speaks volumes about the gravity of our primate interdependency.

In the early days of humans banding together to hunt and gather nomadically, things were a lot less complicated and the roles for men and women pretty clear. The basic physiology of men and women dictated the social participation in principal roles and specific assignments that contributed to the overall support of the social band.

The subsequent domestication of plants and animals and the transition to non-nomadic, agrarian lifestyles marked a key shift. Until the point in human history where nomadic lifestyles were subsumed by static agrarian cultures, the service of masculine energy had been directed primarily toward, and in service to, the intimate feminine interests that surrounded a man's daily life. The land, water, plants, creatures, women and children that a man interacted with on a daily basis were the aspects of the feminine he served and protected through all his masculine efforts. To heap contempt upon the natural rhythms of organic abundance was a detriment not only to his survival, but an affront to what Jung termed as the "anima" or a man's unconscious relationship to his own inner feminine sensibilities.

In the pre-agrarian culture, reverence, wonder and humility all conspired to create a mythology that was deeply rooted to a man's ties to the elements, creatures and community members with whom he conducted his daily intercourse. His actions were attuned to the whole of creation. On a very primal level, he functioned in his actions more as an element of the whole, which mitigated much of what we recognize today as the compartmentalizing of male violence in the modern world. But for our historic male ancestors, things were destined to change. Principally, the rise of central power authority paradigms, the imposition of monetary currency and the introduction of monotheistic religious doctrine in the Middle East would all play a part in the degradation and dismissal of the feminine influences in masculine core expression. Hyper-masculine culture born from this distortion would wreak havoc on the earth for centuries to come, and the error persists today as our ancestral legacy in contemporary forms of human corruption and violence.

The Rise of Central Powers

The shift from nomadic hunter/gatherer cultures to agrarian/industrial (A/I) cultures brings about a shift in the human condition that has ever since given us the mark of the beast. Two elements of this shift impacted core masculine expression greatly. The first element affecting change was the new size of human groupings in A/I social structures, and the second was the new relationship to the environment that A/I culture imposed.

North American indigenous cultures such as the Lakota grouped together in social structures of around 150 or so people (each having its own tribal chief) who were in turn part of the greater Lakota Nation, estimated to be about 20,000 in the mid-18th century. There were reasons for this. Bands of people exceeding these typical amounts were too cumbersome and unwieldy upon the land and resources available naturally to sustain them. Also, at greater numbers, social ties to one another as a clan or tribe began to become compromised as the sense of intimate connectivity to one another within the group fragmented.

A/I cultures, on the other hand, depend on mass populations existing in one area. The fragmentation and loss of relative intimacy compared to nomadic tribal culture are marked. The effect of the loss of intimate connectivity between individuals has deep implications culturally. The most significant implication for A/I cultures is the propensity toward increased intra-communal violence due to a growing individual alienation that diminishes social bonds. The new fragmentation enhances the people's susceptibility to influence by central authority propaganda that may have little allegiance to the community's best interest.

Secondly, agrarian/industrial systems require land and resources to function, but not in the way that nomadic cultures had. Nomadic cultures grew and survived in direct proportion to the sustainable harvesting of what unmanipulated nature had to offer. A/I cultures consumed more resources than were naturally occurring in one area, achieving that result by human modification of the natural environment.

To sustain this kind of social order required an unnatural imposition on the environment, a homogeneous assault on the land and water. Mono-crop cultures, water-flow diversion, damming and channeling of water sources and permanent settlements that required waste disposal strategies as well as protective fortifications all began to erupt everywhere on the land. Transportation infrastructures and housing took root. The capture, breeding and raising of domesticated animals contributed to the already large-scale consumption of land and water resources.

Human beings were now the only living things on the planet that side-stepped the natural order of survival based on naturally occurring abundance, choosing instead to impose mass food production for growing central powers through the labor exploitation of a governed mass of people, domestication of animals for food and utility, and the control and re-engineering of land and water resources.

As social structures developed, expanded and became more

complex, particularly with the move from hunter-gatherer lifestyles to agrarian civilizations, the rise of remote central authority figures such as feudal lords, and fiefdom kings became more commonplace, supplanting community tribal elders and village chiefs who traditionally lived and worked among nomadic people.

These new remote leaders signaled the advent of disconnected central powers that would place demands on the service, allegiance and energetic resources of the average man under such rule. These new rulers governed from a distance, and in this new social paradigm most men served, fought or died for someone they knew only by word of mouth, or perhaps even just through legend.

This new class of rulers were separate creatures, concept figureheads who ruled from behind large walls, away from the everyday toils and struggles of the subjects who served them. This new governing creates a schism in its citizenry because it exists outside of the immediate sphere of intimate proximity to the lives of the majority of men who came to serve those leaders.

At their historical zenith, central power figures became so disconnected from the intimacy of those they governed that a kind of psychic and emotional distortion began to set in. Leaders of large masses such as Pharaohs, Caliphs, Popes, Monarchs and Emperors began to claim divine abstractions of ordained providence particular only to themselves, and in their sovereign isolation became vulnerable to their own self-sanctioned mania.

Derailing of the Masculine

For the masses functioning under the new order of disconnected governing, the rise of the alien ruler gave birth to a kind of socio-mutation that became the first major derailing principle that took men away from organic service to the sacred feminine.

A man's allegiance and life now became devoted to a concept ruler who had no intimate stake or connection to his subjects. This abstract allegiance became an exercise in loyalty to the idea of a distant ruler, supplanting the previous relationship of loyalty to the heart of a leader who had shared and cultivated intimate fraternal bonds with his subjects. This movement was an invitation to the fundamental disconnect that became the keystone to all male violence in the world today. When men began to serve and align their allegiance to conceptual abstractions instead of the heart of another, the real fall of man ensued.

Human beings are unique in their capacity for violent behavior precisely because they alone among earthly creatures can create and react to conceptual paradigms—mere thoughts whose only content may be rooted in pathological fear and distortion. A blind allegiance to the political or religious ideas of some abstract ruler is not a natural alignment for the heart and soul of a man. When the propaganda of disconnected authoritarian rulers like this is taken to be something to be believed and idealized in some kind of fevered frenzy deemed worth fighting and killing over, those concepts become worshipped, as even the Bible says, as "an idol, a false God, a graven image" before God. Here again is born the violence of men, and unfolding from it ever since the horrors and suffering therein.

Ever since the rise of disconnected authority centers, male aggression and apathy have increased exponentially, not just with killing, in times of war. In times of peace, the slow death of empty competition derived from the central power's soulless labor assignments numbs the hearts of men and breeds a morbid apathy. The situation has pressed the masculine sacred devotional capacity further away from its natural integration with the sacred feminine throughout history, so that we find it today having declined into a festering and compartmentalized servitude toward authoritative abstractions, disconnecting men from themselves and a meaningful sense of service in the world.

Currency and the Rise of the Cash Crop

One of the key ways in which central powers initially exacted control over governed masses was through the elimination of traditional, old-style trade-and-barter systems. The imposition of monetized currency by the ruling class ensured that all marketplace activity could be controlled, tracked and taxed by the prevailing central power authorities. This allowed for the forced leveraging of resources from the common man by a disconnected ruling entity that had agendas of power consolidation. Ruling regimes require the support of their subjects. A system of currency makes ruling class resource acquisition available through money taxation while simultaneously augmenting power consolidation through the ability to amass and hoard a valued commodity that does not rot or deteriorate.

The imposition of currency-based systems of commerce has created an unspoken bitterness and simmering mistrust toward central power ruling authorities ever since. Monetary systems have introduced a quietly caustic humiliation that has degraded the dignity of men while abstract rulers covertly bleed off resources from the sweat and labor of those who actually work and produce tangible goods and services. The unresolved festering pathology of the taxed citizen creates a toxic schism in the psyche of the masculine archetype still present today.

The establishment of currency in history concurrently promotes the cultivation of specialized, sometimes non-staple "cash crops" grown in surplus for commercial markets. Currency-based commerce means that money acquisition through the sale of harvests is what now governs agricultural endeavor. The implication is that ranching and farming are no longer locally focused activities where production is geared toward local community consumption needs. This has the devastating effect of wiping out local food crop diversity, and replacing it with a massive mono-crop production of commercial agricultural products destined for a broader market.

The resulting assault on the earth becomes a homogeneous blight on local landscapes. The disruption of local market harmony and the soulless disconnect of laboring for impersonal currency further fragment the community of men from one another. Gone are the days of the direct human exchange of goods and services, as the masculine continues to be further severed from the heart of itself.

The Middle East:
Empires, Conquest and Monotheism

Western civilization is descended from the breadbasket of the Middle East. In America and in Europe, we see the direct historical connection to the influence of these ancient civilizations. The crossroads geography of the Middle East provides several factors that have accelerated the propagation of a succession of competing empires appearing in the region starting from around 1450 BC and extending into the 20th century.

Egyptian, Phoenician, Hittite, Kingdoms of Israel, Assyrian, Babylonian, Persian, Macedonian, Roman, Byzantine, Sassonid, Caliphate, Seljuk, Saladin, Mongol and Ottoman empires (not to mention the Crusades and 20th-century European colonization)—all have known large-scale geographic rule in the region.

In fact, in a period of roughly 3,400 years, the Mediterranean theater sees the rise and fall of nearly 20 enormous empires. No other region in the world can begin to even approach such a remarkable history of varying ethnic regimes arising systematically to consolidate agendas of sweeping conquest on the order and magnitude witnessed in this region throughout history. Cycling through newly established empires at the rate of nearly one every two hundred years, the fertile crescent of the Middle East, North Africa and southern Europe hosted massive campaigns of central power control that ruled over great expanses. These empires must be understood in their scope. Comprising at times in area what would today account in size for perhaps a dozen or more countries in the region, these ancient empires were an astonishing accomplishment of power acquisition and control for their time.

Interestingly, and most notably, the region during this period gave rise to the world's only truly monotheistic religions. Within this hotbed of convulsive military activity, the establishment of monotheistic religious doctrine became essential political grist for social control. The culturing of a people for military aggression and conquest is enhanced with the drawing up of a condoning God that makes the martial agenda a seemingly necessary tonic the masses must follow, and a single male god fits the bill quite nicely. By stripping away from all forms of worship the balancing influence of the divine feminine, an angry, jealous, vengeful and patriarchic god can be utilized to set

37

the social tone for aggressive military agendas of conquest, subjugation and control. In the end it is the monotheistic trifecta of Islam, Judaism and Christianity that will rule the entire region in the modern era.

The single-point, patriarchal god who allowed his "chosen servants" to rule the lives of men with impunity had severely debilitating effects on the tone of generally evolving masculine expression. Men who had been by degree losing connection to life on so many fronts were now forfeiting their sense of wonder and worship for religions that implored them to bow before the angry directives of the self-proclaimed messengers of a totalitarian patriarchal god. God-fearing men were now praying to a vitriolic deity who sounded more like an angry tyrant than any rapture-infused mysterious God of wonder who might create a blade of grass or the celestial heavens above.

With the feminine stripped from the people's practice of worship and wonder, men's hearts began to harden and their capacity for toleration became brittle. Conquest and control through power consolidation were now affirmed and sanctioned from the heavens. The savage actions of power-hungry men had become ordained with a stinging sense of divine righteousness and contempt, and the time was ripe for the absconding of ferocity itself from the common man.

Proprietary Violence

With the rise of central power rulers came their sole claim on the domain of violence. Vengeance, retribution and justice were, at some point in history, wrested from the public and private sectors and taken in as the sole province of a punitive ruling authority.

This action had several affects on masculine expression. Seizing violence from the common man meant an across-the-board domestication of common male ferocity, no matter whether that ferocity was used as a malevolent force or whether it was applied as a protective action in pursuit of legitimate justice.

Strategic acquisition of violence by the ruling class essentially absconded the vessel of fierce aggression that could otherwise have been used to exact vigilante justice or perhaps used ultimately to usurp corrupt central authority power.

Monopolizing violence also allowed the ruling class to put on display in no uncertain terms who owned and controlled the use of force and aggression. Graphic punishment for violators such as whippings, crucifixions, beheadings, floggings, brandings, burnings, breakings, drawing-and-quarterings and the public display of criminal corpses all became instruments of ruling class propaganda, making it viscerally clear to the common man just who was really in charge, while simultaneously striking fear into the hearts of those who might ever contemplate acts of aggression that fell outside of the established rule of law.

Historical statistics from the Middle Ages acknowledge the significant drop in public sector violence starting from around the 15th century. The drop in crime is due to the control of public sector violence through the enforcement of civil order established by the application of codified law and criminal justice, and applied by the rising ruling classes in that period.

The enhancement of relative civility and order cannot be denied, but the absolute seizing and taking of the critical element of physical male aggression on the whole as a proprietary domain of the ruling class has had an interesting effect on the evolving masculine archetype.

Civil aggression, righteous or otherwise, is now transferred to the state and exorcised through the courts and the adversarial criminal justice system, as well as the enforcement arms of government such as the military and police forces. Even today, minimum-force self-defense of the individual may be cautiously provided for in the United States, but lethal use of force is almost unilaterally codified as the strict domain of the state.

There are other less obvious forms of the strategic acquisition and control of male ferocity in the culture that are not so plainly apparent. The harvesting, slaughtering and processing of animals today by huge corporate conglomerates have effectively stolen the hunt as well as the kill from the common man. Men who still hunt or fish for their food have a direct and cellular experience with their prey that can allow for an understanding and appreciation of the balancing virtues of nature. An intimate connection with the animals that one kills and slaughters may ironically cultivate a less volatile and more humble nature in the men who consciously engage in taking the life of those animals they consume as food for sustenance.

Even ranchers raising domestic livestock in healthy and humane ways are by degree being forced out by a bullying monolithic agricultural business that values nothing but quarterly profits. The wisdom and compassion that the intimacy of direct animal husbandry brings to the men who engage in it is something the mechanized and indifferent food processing corporations place no value on.

Many forms of sports activities today provide access to acceptable expression of non-lethal male aggression, but all of these forms ultimately serve a condoning authority that owns, defines, sponsors and controls the violence for entertainment. The Roman Colosseum is alive and well.

What remains to be understood is that common men today are no longer the masters of their own ferocious destiny. Even those who are given the right by authority centers to utilize violence and aggression are given the strict parameters within which it may be conducted.

Ultimately, even the lackeys of today's condoned violence lack the ferocity and quiet authority of the fully realized and liberated masculine core. But perhaps and until men can evolve in a culture that keeps them tracking on a coherent path of masculine expression, it is appropriate that total access to unfettered aggression be taken from them.

But in the long run, if we are to live fully and deeply as men, we must reclaim our archetypal ferocity from human institutions that castrate, sedate and domesticate us from our fierce capacities. In that world however, we as men must have a profound accountability for our full potential as masculine agents in the culture. Before we attempt to reclaim what has been taken from us by central authority powers, we must first learn to serve and submit ultimately to the benevolent will of the Creative Intelligence that sources all things. We may one day be fierce without restraint, but only when that force and power is aligned with and in total allegiance to the benevolent will of the Creator. This in fact was a fundamental message of Jesus Christ, who never lost his sense of ferocity in the face of the abusive central power regimes of his day.

The Enlightenment and Central Power Erosion

It is an essential strategy of central power regimes to negate and dismiss the power of the individual. It has been the role of power-over institutions throughout history to assert that the individual life amounts to very little. For so many centuries the common individual was not valued, not even allowed to emerge from his or her station or class niche to speak up or act to shape history in any significant way. This was the province of the ruling class only, but history again would change things.

Prior to the European Renaissance, governing structure, enforcing order and social policy in Europe were set, controlled and executed by whatever central power figures controlled a particular jurisdiction at that time. Common folk had little access to spare time, education or social resources that would allow for any leverage for them to become much more than the creatures of bare-necessity survival that they were.

The subjective emphasis of the value placed on the individual person (in western culture) likely emerged initially with the Greeks in the age of Aristotle. Before that, a lineage of authority figures, such as those embodied then in the monarchs, high clergy and achievers of vast military conquest, defined and sanctioned the social and cultural content.

But it was during the Renaissance, with the advent of the printing press and institutional centers of education and learning that an ever-growing literacy came to be. This new age catalyzed the proliferation of the polymaths—men of great and diversified learning who gave testimony to a perspective that proclaimed that individuals themselves, with their capacity for reasoning, were the more accurate seat of authentic perception and not the inbred power paradigms of the few central power rulers of the day.

Out of the Renaissance was bred such Age of Reason figures as Francis Bacon and Nicolai Copernicus, who perhaps like no others before them, launched an age of self-derived reason, logic and science that would proceed to inject secular consciousness into the old-world paradigms of religion while intellectually outflanking the aristocracy of the day. Like a viral load too great for its host to bear, science and secular-colored reason began to erode the influence of the central powers of church and monarchy, while simultaneously influencing and inspiring the common man.

The scales began to shift to what historians have described as "Renaissance Humanism," a focus toward the empowerment of the individual in all areas of thought and action. Enlightened souls and great minds emerged to shatter the old ways. Newton, Descartes, Locke, Rousseau, Hume and others all conspired to bring a tidal wave of authority home to the individual for the first time in history, giving rise to a fresh vision of human perspective that took social gravitas away from the central power seats and divine abstractions of the past. For the first time in history the common man was encouraged to consider the suggestion that one's own life destiny is defined by the choices of the individual who lives it.

The titillating notion that the individual man is the compelling center of the Universe grew deep roots, and the novelty of it was intoxicating. A flood of new ideas, insights, innovation and creative brilliance poured into the centuries from 1500 on through the French Revolution. Not until Immanuel Kant did the momentum of this vogue new order of perception begin to feel any kind of real check, challenge or refinement.

Ultimately it was William Blake who brought the whole movement to a coherent crescendo, integrating the best of the empiricists and the rationalists by unfolding it all within the crucible of the ineffable. In his *The Book of Urizen*, Blake lays the bulwark of empiricist thought and rationale at the altar of the eternal essence and exposes the flaws inherent in the Renaissance-induced regime of self-imposed subjective tyranny. Blake reveals that the slave driver is now in our own heads, no less diabolical than the old external despot behind the castle wall.

As for the old school central power paradigms, the damage had been done. Science had trumped the abstractions of dogmatic religion. Ancient Aristotelian reason had refined in the new age to overcome the tainted logic of the self-absorbed aristocracy. Finally the majority of people had access to the printed words of their peers, and grassroots visionaries who inspired through insight, innovation and righteous action set the stage for the mobilization of the masses.

Everywhere in the west, the storm was at the gates of the old guard, and the single-point ruler would soon succumb to the new bourgeois class of intellectual leadership. Behind the front of this new leadership loomed a budding proletariat, a swollen and fevered working class ripe to be propagandized.

The time was at hand for men to create a new cultural paradigm that represented a divergence with the past; it was time to experiment with a new order of social governing. In the American colonies, the window of opportunity seemed perfectly suited to just such a revolution. A handful of relatively affluent colonists began to coalesce around the idea, and drawing on the high ideals of the best minds from the Renaissance, they put pen to paper and blood to soil to bring about the American Revolution.

MEN AND THE AMERICAN EXPERIMENT

Shadows and shallow breaths
Lives lived faintly
Through dreamy deaths.
Begging to see
With eyes shut tight
Deliverance from
Our chosen night.

— From *Shadows and Shallow Breaths*

American Me

What will define a nation of people are its laws, its tradition and its culture. In many ways I am a product of the American experiment.

A culture is expressed through its people. Law is the father of culture, and tradition is the ancestors. We now express as individual men a culture that our fathers told us was appropriate by virtue of the law, and they in turn were handed down the spirit of that law through the conveyed traditional values of their ancestors.

Culture, law and tradition—these conspire to make the expressive dimension of a man in today's world. As American men, we have our own unique legacy to understand and integrate. As men in America it is our responsibility to understand just what it is that has shaped us—how law, culture and tradition have conspired to influence exactly who we are today.

Law

Many imagine that our laws have come down to us from some high-minded council of social scholars, individuals who have codified their superior insights into splendid legal doctrines meant to guide the common masses through a life of order and sanity. Indeed, law ought to give men the structural conduit through which a coherent life can flow. It should protect and encourage the best in a culture of people and ought to hold men accountable to a standard of true conduct and coherent action.

The unfortunate reality here in America is that law is either decreed or legislated by those in seats of isolated power. In spite of the rhetoric in American politics that spins the illusion that lawmakers are here to represent us by benevolently protecting and nurturing what is best for us as a people, that is often not the case.

The Declaration of Independence was this nation's founding legal doctrine. It is a document that initially served to encourage a diverse people to unite and come together under one cause worth fighting for, against the most powerful nation on earth at the time. Such a document would, by necessity, need to be highly inspired material.

Landed gentry and local government officials of the day came together as a congress of concerned American colonists and conspired to find a way to convince rural farmers to fight a war that the landed gentry would create. They needed a creative strategy.

They found insight in the great Enlightenment thinkers of the recent past. They utilized the influence of colonial patriots such as Thomas Paine, Patrick Henry and Paul Revere, and drew upon their spirit to steer the creation of a Declaration that would embody those grassroots sentiments and stir a diverse citizenry into extreme action: a revolutionary war.

After the American Revolution, the new government was established and the nation settled into its infancy. But very quickly, laws began to be generated that served not the whole people who had fought for the new nation, but instead benefited the affluent few. The new idealistic nation was quickly morphing into a government of the capitalists, by the capitalists and for the capitalists.

The fact is that American law was founded by colonial capitalists of that period and has continued to this day to be controlled by contemporary capitalists who are not interested in inciting grassroots revolution. On the contrary, legislation created after the Bill of Rights served to build a newly founded nation in the interests of the power players who found themselves at the head of the new nation. Those power brokers were primarily the founding capitalists who had run the American war for independence, subsequently followed by the next generation of new money barons who had emerged from the economic boom cycle of the industrial revolution here in America.

Post-Revolution law in America has traditionally been more an instrument of capitalist power centers consolidating power and less an engine of the framers' stirring idealism for personal freedom and empowerment. The original spirit of the law in this country may point to and suggest authentic human expression at the constitutional level, but in practice, and unfortunately, in too much of the subsequent broader codified and common law created after the Bill of Rights, it does not. Big money leverages and shapes legislative action in Congress and in state legislatures, and very few average citizens have the time, inclination or understanding to keep on top of the shady dealings.

Because of this, very little law generated outside of the original Constitution supports authentic masculine expression. The practice and legislation of law today generally nurtures division, not equality. It tends to serve agendas, not liberty. For the most part, it is beholden to special interests, not viable cultural traditions. Law in reality has become ultimately an instrument of the affluent, and not necessarily an accessible safeguard of the common.

The American legal system, particularly at the judicial level, has become an adversarial dog-and-pony show, where self-serving agendas, cloaked in the image of high concepts and scholarly language, strut and fret upon the stages of justice. Out of these dramatic courtroom exhibitions we can justifiably ask how often the common man has come out the better for it, relative to the time, resources and energy put in.

Ironically for us here in America, the die that was cast in the Declaration of Independence and the Bill of Rights has continued to foment emphatic notions of equality, liberty and justice through the centuries since. That this country is actually about liberty, justice and freedom is the curious deception that cannot be put to rest; it has become the dirty little lie that must be perpetuated in the American seats of economic power to prevent unsettled masses from moving toward whole-scale dissent, revolution or anarchy. What we as an American people may see in the Declaration and Bill of Rights as the fundamental spirit of our land, capitalists tend to see as merely a soothing propaganda that is best left in place to give the appearances of benevolent action at governmental seats of power, even though they are offices that ultimately serve as puppets to the big-money interest groups that control them.

In tandem with corrupt legislation we also find so much time is wasted judicially with frivolous lawsuits of greed and petty special interests that end up ultimately generating laws that pander to the lowest common denominator of human idiocy. These legal mechanisms are not producing the structural conditions required of a healthy male culture; indeed they are shattering the masculine core.

What law is there then for us as American men to ground our lives in as a people? What does the myriad of codified chaos found in the unending string of statutes, codes, regulations and ordinances mean to us intimately as a people today? How does law in this nation intimately touch our heart and spirit in such a way as to help shape us as men?

Perhaps the framers of the Constitution were inspired men, idealistic individuals not confined to a cumbersome and perhaps flawed tradition of traditional government. Maybe they believed in the idealistic precepts they codified and put their names to; they may have indeed been men who were ahead of their time. But Jefferson did not have his 10-year cyclic revolution dreams realized here in America. Since our nation was born, there has been no recurring radical and serious examination here of the central powers that govern and shape our lives.

For the generations after the American Revolution it has been just another separate ruling class power that has settled in to evolve the law of the land through the influence and manipulation of elected government officials. Do we really have a tradition of freedom or merely a pretense of noble intention?

Tradition

The founding idealisms of freedom, liberty and equality do not serve because they have become mostly abstractions, rather than a congruent value affirmed, emphasized and pressed into the culture in a concrete way. Aside from the night-sky spectacle of the 4th of July, where and when do we all express, celebrate and ritualize this nation's founding principles in a communal and coherent way?

Perhaps the high-minded notions of freedom and independence that the framers put forth have met historically with too much national hypocrisy to try and seriously celebrate. As a budding nation we may have wrestled away from a colonial empire, but we in turn simply became an empire ourselves. We codified notions of equality, freedom and liberty, but for nearly a century after, among other things, utilized slave labor in this country. We have preached about a government "by the people, of the people and for the people" in a land where the people are being routinely depleted and oppressed by systemic government corruption at every level of office. Out of this current situation it is understandable that no coherent national tradition has comprehensively taken hold.

In the United States at large, an encompassing tradition is hard to locate where so many disparate ethnic and religious groups vie for majority influence. With so much diversity in the social landscape and rampant corruption in the political structures, no singular tradition presents itself to establish predominating customs that might unify the country throughout. Without a unifying tradition underlying the people of the United States, we are left with a cultural vacuum that embodies no real established heritage.

Into this vacuum has stepped the capitalist propaganda regime, defining tradition in terms of a cleverly crafted and intensely perpetuated national consumerism. Our traditions are now mostly revealed in the common consumption of name-brand products and trademark services. A doctrine of unbridled product and service acquisition has become the American creed.

Men are left to fend for themselves amid a competitive labor market where they must do whatever it takes to place themselves in a respectable position of at least traditional consumption standards. This, they are told, is the path to success. This is what we as men are given as an American tradition.

Culture

The fact that America lacks a definitive and comprehensive tradition means that there is no foundation from which a coherent culture can arise and take hold. Art, music and literature are ever-increasingly the domain of media propagation, again in the hands of the capitalist oligarchy. What gets published, aired, played and performed is increasingly the instrument of capitalist propaganda actualized through self-serving marketing.

Even the advent of the internet has so far failed to produce the hoped-for fountainhead of pure artistic expression that supercedes mainstream market-driven product. Indeed, the World Wide Web has become just another cauldron from which the cream can rise, only to be then harvested by the producers of economic gain. Our artists, our teachers, our performers and our men are routinely the homogeneous spawn of venture capital. As such, the potential rainbow color of a dynamic culture is ever processed by economic forces into a monochromatically muted gray. It is in this culturally barren environment that men have become docile, passive and content to have their piece of the pie and fit tidily into the packaged products they are assigned to be.

Law, Tradition, Culture and Men

Without law that is designed to serve and protect the people it governs, no nation is safe or truly free enough to cultivate or propagate authentic masculine expression within its borders. Laws that bolster agendas outside of its people's national interest will eventually consume its citizenry.

Without an encompassing tradition that passes a nation's time-tested wisdom from one generation to another within a comprehensive crucible of benevolent unity, no true fraternal order of men will be encouraged to arise. In such an environment of vacant acumen, all the history of folly and suffering of men will simply repeat itself.

Without a culture that values and fosters beauty, integrity, understanding and intelligent action, a people cannot cultivate the intuition that brings men close to the heart of life. Our muses will be false idols, and our artists will fail in their ability to invite us toward the inspired content of our own souls.

Understanding the social fabric of American life may shed more light on exactly why we currently, as a people, have a deficit of authentic men in our midst.

The Industrial Revolution

Colonial America was initially a rural agrarian state. The American Revolution ended on the heels of the explosively new industrial revolution, and the shift from rural agrarian lifestyles to urban-focused manufacturing centers took hold in the young nation. The transition brought rural citizens in search of employment flocking into urban centers of manufacturing and commerce, coupled with waves of immigrants from other countries.

Getting men acclimated to working long hours in cramped, dark and uncomfortable factories was an awkward transition at first. These men were accustomed to the rhythms of agrarian labor. Agrarian work was mostly out-of-doors in the fresh air and involved a man engaged in a variety of tasks and skill sets. Factory work was indoors, singular, dull and repetitive. Also, urban labor rewarded currency, printed or coined money that could be exchanged for the kind of produce that rural living often simply provided through the harvesting at farms and ranches. The intimacy around the pure exchange of trade and barter was being replaced by the cavalier abstractions of a promissory note.

The industrial shift took men off farms and ranches and put them in cities and in crowded workplaces. It took them away from the solar rhythms of the day and had them working hours well beyond the setting sun. It broke apart the bonds that a husband and wife forged in the day-to-day, side-by-side struggle for survival. It took fathers away from their daughters and their sons. It drove men away from each other and created desperate and fragmented competitive environments where no one won except the capitalist employer.

This new brand of soulless urban work could grind a man down to a mean despair, and make him beholden to something even more brutal than the familiar man versus nature circumstances of agrarian subsistence. Suddenly the theater of labor action had changed from man versus nature to man versus man. Men now worked for other men and were fighting with each other for the limited available jobs. The formula was simple: working-class men served entitled men with land and factories who had access to capital. The average man now labored for monetary compensation paid to him by entitled men with capital. The agrarian struggle against the elements and the fickle ways of nature were nothing compared to what most men confronted now: an insulated and privileged opponent they called an employer.

Behind the scenes, encouraged capitalists entreated the halls of government to create mandatory institutions that might indoctrinate the mass of American children into sitting quietly in one place for hours and hours every day while learning to work for extrinsic reward. The government complied with the need and the American public school system was born, which would graduate every year new waves of docile factory workers. Arguably, the new program of public school education had its benefits and its well-intentioned promoters, but it is important to understand that institutionalized education for the general population of youth in America was born the day family structures were torn apart by the post-industrial revolution era, when fathers were pulled away from their homes in pursuit of wage labor assignments.

Horace Mann, the chief architect of the American public school system, declared unabashedly his intentions through public education to instill values such as obedience to authority, and promptness in attendance. He wished to create upright republican citizens out of the virtually fatherless unruly children of the mid-1800s. Students would learn, among other things, to respond to the organizing prompts of bell ringing, preparing them for the authoritatively directed environment of future employment.

These publicly educated kids became the new breed of socially engineered young adults who had been conditioned for years as children to stay in one place, behave and do what they were told by unrelated authority figures and do it all for whatever reward (or punishment) those figures offered. What is more, information packaged as remedial education could be distorted, shaped with propaganda and utilized to create values and belief systems that affected social consciousness.

It all seemed to be working great for the well-to-do. The rich were getting richer and the poor were staying that way—that is until the working class began to unite in the late 19th century. By then, the subsuming of male labor from mainstream agrarian lifestyles into urban wage earners had been well-established. The average American male was no longer an active member of his own household, and the implications were staggering.

With an exhausted father at some remote location of labor activity and the sons in school being educated/indoctrinated, no real transmission from father to son of how to be in the world as a man could occur. Fathers/husbands became despondent, isolated, mean and empty with rote industrial labor assignments, while boys became packaged products of the state's so-called educational program. Wives and mothers of the day suffered quietly, disoriented by the domestic degradation of the deepening fragmented family structure. Left at home alone, literally abandoned, women helplessly watch as their husbands and their children were fed to the new industrial capitalist machine. The next devolution of social structure had arrived, driving men farther away from the masculine core than ever before.

Capitalists versus the American Proletariat

The age of the industrial capitalists had created yet another class system to replace the old. Aristocracy was out, and the capitalists were in. Rural peasants were out, and the new working class proletariat was in. Slavery was out, and exploitative sub-poverty-level wages were in.

With the onset of a wage-labor society, the family unit had been shattered. The keystone of all fundamental human bonding and connection became so devastatingly disintegrated that fathers no longer had the opportunity to influence their sons (or their daughters) the way they had in agrarian times. Domestic bonds were threadbare, functioning with just the narrowest forms of family intimacy and cohesion. This domestic fragmentation diminished community connection and solidarity, making any functional resistance to oppression a very remote possibility.

But for the capitalists, another challenge to their totalitarian grip arose. The oppressive labor conditions and exploitative wages of the times began to catalyze the persistent archetypal tendency of men toward fraternal bonding, in this case under the common cause of suffering. The harsh wage and labor circumstances served to stimulate a new rising order of fraternal camaraderie, the American labor union.

From the late 19th century on through the mid-20th century, labor unions struggled to correct the capitalist stranglehold on wages, labor conditions and worker rights. The labor union cause consumed the country's best and most courageous men in the battle to neutralize capitalist tyranny over the common man. Labor union efforts at the zenith of union power struck fear into the capitalist elite. Through massive solidarity, the unions achieved milestone accomplishments, with rights and wages being affected in mainstream industry throughout many areas of the country.

The economic power players responded by further leveraging the government to crack down with legislation, high court precedent and police state enforcement. But ultimately the sheer numbers of union solidarity, bolstered by recent socialist reformation thinkers such as Lenin and Marx, began to demonstrate potentially paralyzing control on U.S. commerce, albeit in localized areas of the country.

In one such strike, originating in Seattle, Washington, in 1919, the entire city and ports ground to a halt for nearly a week. What is more, the sheer volume of manpower and union solidarity participating in the walkout was so massive that union officials decided to utilize the force to benevolently fend off anarchy and chaos in the streets by distributing food through the infrastructure they now controlled. For the U.S. government and the industrial money barons, the whole-scale success and grassroots support of the incident were disturbing and bore too many similarities to the recent Bolshevik Revolution in Russia; the oligarchy demagogues were beginning to get concerned.

The power elite, with names like Mellon, Carnegie, Morgan and Rockefeller, had little faith in the government's singular capacity to control the rising political tide of socialist reform in America by mere police state enforcement. But in 1929, the country was brought to its knees with a stock market crash that put the country into an economic vice that over time crushed union solidarity. Not until WWII would the general economy of the United States really begin to recover.

The post-WWII era allowed capitalists, again through government propaganda, to utilize the brutish agenda of Soviet dictator Joseph Stalin as justification to formulate a "Red Scare" that would terrorize the residual strongholds of the socialist and communist labor movement in the United States. The capitalists had grown wealthier with the defeat of the axis powers of Europe, and now they had vanquished the labor unions of America. Even though the unions were allowed to remain as part of the American economic landscape, they would never again wield the power to bring U.S. commerce to its knees.

As icing on the cake, a bold new strategy was to be undertaken by the money elite; they would initiate the creation of a sedated American "middle class" to buffer dissent. Men who were powerless but content would populate the new middle class. The new drug of the masses would be material acquisition of consumer goods, the perfect recipe for a consumerism culture. What families could not afford to buy with cash, they would be encouraged to purchase with a new profitable control device called credit.

The mid-20th century was the age of the social lobotomy in the United States, and American men fell in line like lemmings. The media sounded the trumpet for the good life, and the new age of leisure and material acquisition began to unfold. But within a generation something unanticipated would arrive. A bogus war, a deluge of psychedelic street drugs, archetypal music, mass access to college and a lot of free time would bring on something the money elites never saw coming. Welcome to the counterculture movement of the 1960s.

Counterculture and the
Feminist Stopgap

By the mid-1950s, a lumbering and disconnected masculinity had taken on the look and feel of a rote and dimensionless patriarchal culture. Mass media was king. Radio and television bombarded the ears and eyes of the masses daily. Mid-century masculine media icons such as Errol Flynn and John Wayne were beginning to lose their one-dimensional appeal. A new breed of brooding masculine expression was seeping into the media through anti-heroes like James Dean and Marlon Brando. Emboldened by the space and freedom afforded by the apparently prosperous times of the brand-new middle class, a fresh generation of male youth began to peel away from the tired and stale tradition of rugged individualism that their fathers had embraced.

By the mid-1960s a politically contrived war in Vietnam, civil rights struggles here at home, drugs, rock-and-roll music and unprecedented college enrollment had all conspired to raze the social structures of the worn-out male paradigms. The deep prevailing rift between the educated youth and the old male guard that led up to the counterculture movement of the '60s also fed the adroit feminist recoil forever immortalized as "women's liberation."

Yet the new feminist movement was hardly about any renaissance of the true feminine archetype. Women may have been "liberated" in some ways during the '60s and '70s from the limitations imposed on them throughout history by the flawed masculine, but they were hardly set free into their core feminine. Indeed, the feminist reaction became a drastic and blunt resignation of the trust the feminine had put into the unskillful and utterly lost male guard that for so long had been running the culture.

As a result, women began to turn away from many forms of male interdependency. To compensate for the external male deficiency in their lives, women themselves started taking on those aspects of the masculine. Drive, initiative, aggression and linear activation in the world began to preempt a feminine emphasis in the so-called liberated woman. In doing this it appeared that a woman could make her own way without having to marry into the masculine polarity.

These women pressed their freshly cultivated masculinity into their dominant expression, contrary to their innate impulse to express their feminine as dominant. An appalled patriarchal culture took to calling these women "ball-busters" or even "bitches" for outflanking their piously hollow masculinity, but the true accountability for the feminist maneuvering in the first place was all ours as men. Had we provided a healthy masculine opportunity for these women to couple with, the suffering and mistrust that drove the feminist movement would have never arisen.

The feminist movement in turn created the arising of an opportunistic creature I call the "soft male," which wended its parasitic way into the liberation movement. The soft male suppresses or sidesteps a full masculine expression and cultivates a feminine emphasis against his natural impulses, and the combination of soft males and the newly liberated woman often finds refuge in one another. However, what is achieved in the feminist/soft-male pairing is little more than an unnatural gender polarity reversal.

In the end, many "liberated" feminist women grew jaded, in some cases becoming as hard and tyrannical as profane men; and the soft manipulative, opportunistic males who bonded with them unsurprisingly fell short of the requisite masculine potency that makes for effective men in the culture.

Women of all ages today actually desire a return to a feminine emphasis; that movement does not necessarily arise as nostalgia for pre-counterculture female roles. The liberation movement has gifted the context of choice to women today. The hour of desperation is over because women have learned to survive toxic male environments without depending on men to bail them out. Even if it is done at a certain cost, women know they can outflank the existing male hegemony. The difference is that today, they are less willing to trade off their feminine emphasis to do it.

Today's Virtual Exchange

The last 30 years have offered very little in the way of significant cultural events that have served to change core masculine expression in the United States. Perhaps the most profound contemporary impact on human relations in general can be found with the advent of the computer culture and the introduction of the internet into international platforms of social interconnectivity.

It is estimated today that a billion people around the world use the internet, a full one-sixth of the planet's total human population. Just considering that so much of humanity can access and interact instantly with each other has deep implications for the human condition, and computer-based interconnectivity is just beginning to reveal many intriguing insights into the nature of human relationship.

It is an exceedingly interesting time. In America, the age we find ourselves in is one driven by what truly amounts to a whole-scale, intra-psychic disconnect coupled with the mass interconnectivity of the internet, and the irony is almost amusing were it not so tragically revealing.

The World Wide Web has exponentially accelerated our capacity to access other people and information, but the greater access has not necessarily translated to better quality, on either count. Like any other power-enhancing resource, the internet only magnifies what is already present in the content of the user. If we as a collective community of people are lost, disoriented, disconnected and confused, the internet will mostly serve to turn up the volume on those conditions by broadcasting our capacity to express them.

Who is quite decidedly being affected most in our culture by computers is our youth. Unlike those of us born before the 1980s, internet-bred youth have less and less experience cultivating relationships directly and in person. For masculine evolution, this is another huge step in the wrong direction. More alienation, more self-absorption and a morbidly apathetic disconnect are quietly building momentum in the younger generations.

The actual act of directly relating in person appears to have become a source of odd irritation to America's youth. The direct accountability of in-person relating has become a relative nuisance compared to the insulation and titillation of the disembodied chat that occurs in cell phone texting, and computer-based messaging, chat rooms and other computer-based social media.

These cyber-social forms of communication exchange lack the in-person elements of expressing and receiving that have been inherent in all communication from time immemorial. In the new communication paradigm, the appearance of less risk and less accountability bolsters false notions of boldness and connection. With social media, there is no need to demonstrate a quality of presence to your audience because you are talking through an insulating firewall of technology that can assure anonymity in many cases.

There is an alarming vacancy of content with human interaction over these mediums. Interestingly enough, even with easy and free access to web-cam audio/visual communications over the internet, most of contemporary users prefer the anonymity of chat rooms instead. Hiding behind a cyber veil allows a daringness of thought and speech that would never arise with in-person accountability.

For the entire male culture in general, and for young men particularly, these contemporary forms of relating affect intimacy skills, with self and with others. The organic tension of interpersonal relations necessitates a course of self-intimacy as it builds the required character to achieve its end. The gravitas of direct person-to-person exchange summons an authentic expression not present in virtual communications.

There is no risk in breathing fire in a chat room. Damning your cyber enemies or falling in cyber-love become hollow acts of zero content until actual living personal relations are engaged. Yet here we are with the emergence of social media Casanovas and gamer-heroes, in an electronic dreamscape, where an individual doesn't even have to leave his bed to "feel" like a champion, because he's virtually on top of the world.

The implication of this on our social fabric is staggering, and it has yet to fully impact the culture. Once the pre-internet, pre-cell phone generation dies off, much of the wisdom around relational intimacy and healthy interpersonal risk may die off with it. Because

Generation X is the last generation raised in an environment prior to computers and cell phones, it has by necessity learned essential interpersonal intimacy skills at a young developmental age that the advent of the cell phone and internet age has blighted.

One may wonder whether these lost, basic skill sets might even be marketable to the generations that follow. What my generation takes for granted with respect to basic interpersonal communication may, in the end, turn out to be an important language that quietly falls into obscurity.

We can only hope that the internet will become less about trying to find connection and a meaningful relationship and more about being a repository of information that will be a pointer to where those organic experiences can be found in actual life.

True transmission of wisdom and authentic relationship exchange can occur only in the experience of being in the direct personal presence of the embodied source you are relating with. The rich nuances of interpersonal transmissions that are essential elements of face-to-face exchange are rendered flat, soulless and unintelligible in typed words over a screen. Posturing in chat rooms can never cultivate the essential masculine virtues that build potent men.

We can only hope that, come what may in this world, the deep current of the masculine archetype will always pull at men's hearts and yearn to be embodied and actualized with blood and sweat, instead of with an energy drink and a keyboard. For when our brave new cyber-world ends up producing little more then the post-modern distillation of some painfully empty feeling that twists in the gut, then we as men can take that as a clear message from the wisdom of our bodies that it may be time to step away from the computer for a while, and maybe try gazing into a good old-fashioned sunset instead of the pale, pasty glow of a computer screen.

5

EARLY MALE STAGES
AND INITIATION

Smoke on the horizon
Brings a change
And nothing's the same.

And all our love
Becomes the fuel
That feeds the flame.

— From *Don't Fade Away*

Adolescence

The obscuring of masculine archetypal wisdoms, along with the loss of the critical male initiation ritual in adolescent males, has had devastating effects in this culture. Not only are adult men currently disoriented and confused, but the masculine essence as a whole has failed to evolve for some time. The loss of ritual initiation has given rise to an error that ultimately centers around the lack of skillful integration regarding the powerful utility of individual mortality, cultural duty and communal connection—all critical leveraging aspects of adolescent male rites of passage.

In effect, a young man must learn to straddle paradoxes. He must learn early on an art that will require him to marry in himself emptiness with fullness, stillness with activation, the unknown with the known, power with powerlessness, the divine with the purely mortal. Death proximity through ritual rite of passage becomes an essential element that forges the fusion of these paradoxes within the young male psyche.

This elemental initiation is critical for a male youth because his budding identity is so unintegrated. The lack of integration is due to his relative nearness to the event of conception and incarnation into a body form. Youthful men feel the vitality that is sourced from the immense crucible of the creative matrix from whence they have just recently emerged. Youthful "puer" energy, as Jung referred to it, has very little awareness of limitation, lack, powerlessness, structure or mortality.

Youth-intoxicated perception needs an incarnation adjustment for a solid masculine foundation to take a healthy form. This was traditionally accomplished in tribal cultures through the ritualized rites established in the passage of adolescence. These ritualized events present to the initiate a symbolic facing down of the fear of death itself while engaging in a structured duty assignment. The assigned task invites the willingness of the young initiate to put his precious new life on the line for the greater good of the community he belongs to.

Such rituals almost always involve a task executed by the initiate for the benefit of the community at large. It is a mission designed to bring the neophyte male into an intimate awareness of the sense that his own death could be imminent, yet the duty toward communal service must serve to trump the fear. In the face of these ritualized social undertakings, the young man's cultural immersion will serve to bring about the compelling sense of community connection from which he accesses the epic courage, power and fierceness to embrace his own mortality while forging his individual sense of efficacy and purpose.

Often the ancestral spirits are called upon to assist the young neophyte in his particular endeavor, further consolidating his ties to the heritage and cultural momentum of his people. Such ritualized rites of passage press into participation the conscious power of the whole community to help thrust the individual over the threshold of his young narcissistic tendency toward self-preservation.

The crucial event will precipitate a context where the young man will make a very intimate and critically profound choice that will transform him forever; he will either shrink away from his ritual responsibility in fear of significant harm or discomfort occurring to his personal well-being or he will accept and embrace whatever fate may arise from the full execution of the ritual endeavor in the name of, and for the sake of, the whole community he is a part of. If he chooses the latter and fulfills his culture's expectations in the face of potential harm or death, he will consolidate within himself the initial foundation that will prepare him for the coming life events that continue to forge his true masculine core.

Once again, it is essential to emphasize that the masculine core will find true fulfillment only in the act of putting the whole before the individual, sparking the sense of service and coherent connection that is essential to the masculine archetype. Having achieved this milestone, the young, neophyte man will find in himself the raw and fierce power of the foundational masculine at his center.

This power ultimately translates to the providing for and protection of his community in general and his family in particular. At this stage a young man feels very little sense of lack or limitation. He is primed for a life of coherent contribution. He has the requisite passion and is ready to embark on the difficult journey of life before him.

The relative imbalance of youthful exuberance over middle-aged wisdom will actually serve him well as a neophyte, for at this point on his journey he would do better to not understand fully the overwhelming scope of challenges he will need to rise to in a life fully lived. In time, as the young man's journey ripens, the blind spots of the puer archetype will become reconciled with age and experience.

Existing Cultural Forms of Initiation

A general lack of wisdom in our culture regarding these critical adolescent passages has left a serious void in the social structure that our youth emerge from. Young men cannot be stripped of their archetypal urges, but a culture can lose its capacity to wisely engage and nurture such expression. Such is the case in our social fabric today.

Our young men launch out with youthful velocity into a social order that is not fully prepared to receive them. The primal impulses of these boys explode out into a culture that fails to qualify those raw qualities—decade after decade. Without the proper transformative rites of passage held within a crucible of adult male wisdom, young men will unconsciously seek a default form of expression or outlet.

Many such young men will attempt to substitute the full-scope experience of male adolescent rites by indulging in sophomoric activities that provide a euphoric adrenaline thrill without any of the content that ritual forms include. These activities are the junk-food version of ritual initiation and typically involve a calculated potential risk activity without elder guidance or appropriate community participation. These rudderless adventure-seeker exploits hardly mimic the full experience and scope of meaningful action that occur in the rite-of-passage ritual that traditional initiation with community sanction provides.

These stand-in fillers also lack in their ability to break the egotistical posturing that is common in adolescents, and so the immature male will remain then in his self-serving mode, failing to evolve into the true masculine core. The omission of any real communal connection in relation to the act of risk fails to manifest the essential service-to-duty component that is the heart of the masculine doctrine.

The temptation later on in life to indulge power-over dynamics will be strong in such uninitiated men. The void they will come to feel inside resulting from a lack of true masculine core development and integration will drive them to attempt to fill that emptiness with the false sense of potency that is derived from controlling strategies. A woman's trust, heart and body can often become prey for such imbalanced men.

A man who has not consciously reconciled his own mortality and submitted his will and service toward the greater good of his culture's best interest through proper ritual initiation is not yet ripe for bonding with the feminine, because he is diminished in his capacity to serve the culture at large.

Amish Rumspringa

Young men moving from adolescence to manhood require an interesting mix of structure and freedom. To coddle a boy at this stage is to undermine his own masculine power potential by discouraging his access to it. To impose too much directive control over his life will

71

squelch and distort his core masculine expression by devolving it. Interestingly enough, in my opinion, the Amish manage to accomplish the worst of both worlds through the locally ritualized adolescent passage they refer to as Rumspringa.

The relative self-imposed isolation of the Amish community allows for a powerfully closed context within which to rear children. But the wholesale dismissal and rejection of so many aspects of the diversely modern culture all around them provide for a peculiar distortion that is intensely guarded in a womb-like social structure mired in a stubbornly inert tradition.

Out of this context comes the Amish rite of Rumspringa, during which both male and female adolescents who reach 16 years of age are allowed to unabashedly explore and engage an outside world they have very little understanding of. At this time Amish youth can taste the life offered by the non-Amish culture usually consisting of the heretofore unfamiliar indulgencies of drugs, alcohol and sex. If the children choose to go off and explore outside the culture, they have little support from their parents or community if they do so; they are living a sort of exile during this period. After experiencing the carnal adventures of Rumspringa, Amish youth can then decide for themselves whether or not they want to return and commit to a lifetime of Amish communal living.

In this instance there is no preparation, no guidance and no real meaning to the rite of passage aside from the punitively implied and disfigured message that life outside of the Amish world is no life at all. But the whole affair is not really about embodying any rite of social passage toward healthy adulthood; it is instead a set-up for failure.

Rarely can the young Amish adolescents fully integrate the point-blank experience of the outside social structures they are about to enter. The Amish set the age of exposure at 16, where there is little chance that the undeveloped psyche will be able to cope. This increases the chances that the adolescents will return to the community with their tails between their legs. The process is brutally destructive to the developing psyche of the young teens who venture out on Rumspringa. The event can become a trauma they may never fully process in their lives as adults.

Too much confining structure only to move abruptly into absolute abandonment is not a recipe for healthy young adult integration. Rumspringa exploits the fragility of adolescent developmental stages to manipulate an agenda that achieves a certain end. Rumspringa functions like a preemptive leveraged control of its young Amish members, manipulating them toward a retention of lifetime commitment to Amish ways. A healthy social structure does not abandon or exploit adolescent developmental needs.

Gangs as Proxy
Fraternal Bonding

A society that does not provide culturally sanctioned rites of passage for young men will likewise not produce structures for any coherent order of adult fraternal bonding. The fact that there exists such a key social deficit does not mitigate the raw archetypal urge for fraternal connection inherent in most men. Men need to cooperate with one another regularly. It is essential that men remain consistently lubricated in the practice of working together toward goals that enhance cultural well-being.

The fulfillment of core fraternal bonding needs cannot be fully met by our culture's shallow employment offerings, and typical off-hour activities such as bowling leagues, football Sundays and poker games will only serve to moderately ease the tension that builds behind such an essential unmet core need in men. This is why alcohol or marijuana is so often associated with the many free-form activities men choose to proxy in place of activities that promote fully realized fraternal communion. The diffusive buzz that alcohol or pot provides often helps cloud the nagging sense of incompleteness and unease around most superficial male bonding.

For some men, the fire behind the need for deep fraternal bonds can become fierce. Such men will not be content passing time at the corner pub with their barstool posse. There are men who are dead serious about the depth and dependability of the camaraderie that they will forge with other men. These are men who will seek blood bonds that can withstand any test of loyalty and devotion. Such men will often end up either heroes or criminals in a social structure that simply cannot accommodate their intense drive for a no-bullshit brotherhood that withstands any and all compromises to commitment and dedication.

For young men hungry for this more intense order of fraternal unity, traditional contemporary society has little to offer. Bonds forged in combat never lie, and young men intuitively know this. As a result, ethnic street gangs, motorcycle band affiliations and prison brotherhoods often provide the seemingly straight-up, real deal for men willing to put it all on the line for their fraternal order. Many of the men in these brotherhoods, I believe, could have heroic proportion if it were not for the petty and destructive intentions of control and domination that support various criminal element activities of the gangs they populate.

These groups emphasize one thing above all else, and that is loyalty. In such contexts, betraying a fellow member in particular, or the brotherhood in general, can mean a death sentence or worse. The stakes are high, the commitment is all-in, and the fierce power of the collective order can be intense and intoxicating. Yet group consecrations that merely pander to individual social status or money instead of life-affirming action simply cannot provide a powerful enough context for men to go to a depth of masculine potential that is truly fulfilling.

This is why even the extreme criminal brotherhoods lack a full integration of the true masculine core as I define it. The essential commitment of duty to a life of service that is dedicated to life-enriching action is absent in these groups. The effect here is that power in criminal fraternal orders is drawn primarily from the individual personality of each member, and from there utilized within a collective force of duty-bound individuals. While this can be formidable in some physical applications of forceful coercion, such action can never achieve the heroic proportions of men who have transcended their own self-serving nature for a life of service to the greater good of all.

One who serves all of life has access to the immense power of the life current that flows out of the primordial creative force. Such a man is not limited to the small potentials of the subjective personality structure, whether expressed individually or in groups. This is why the intention and purpose of male fraternal orders will either limit or liberate the capacities of masculine activation potential.

It is clear that violence will always follow self-serving agendas. Violence will always follow group agendas not consecrated to benevolent action that considers the whole. No man can actualize the broad and potent expression of the full masculine core when his allegiance is pledged to a narrow form of functioning. In order for men to express fully, they must live deeply. The full current of life power will not move full-throttle through an un-actualized masculine instrument.

We may conclude that it is not so much that men are violent by intention, but that they have simply become dangerously volatile by the confusion and error of the misguided social programming they are immersed in. Men have adopted the flawed social options available to them to express their power, and we need not totally condemn them for those choices—because those choices are what the culture has provided for them, depending in particular on who they are and where they have come from.

When I did work inside prisons with the inmates there, we had direct and frank discussions about the nature of male power and full core masculine strength. For example, killing another man because he "dissed" you was often perceived as a sign of male power within these circles. In these cases I would often invite a discussion regarding the capacity of a man to create space in his choices before employing lethal force. Was a life reduced to long-term incarceration really worth a few petty words of disrespect? How much freedom and power does a man really embody when he simply reacts and cannot make clear, grounded choices regarding the application of punitive force?

When we do not judge the violent act of personal retribution itself, we may look at the broader scope of considerations about what male potency truly is in moments such as these. I found that convicts could relate to this line of inquiry, because it was not an attempt to castrate them or mitigate their ferocity as men; it was instead a legitimate questioning regarding the choice about undertaking the particular action that was defined as criminal.

We must make individual men aware of their true nature and what they require to fulfill it. When it comes to strategies of evolution and change of the masculine core, it is prudent and necessary to provide for men potent social choices that are beyond contempt, choices that are readily accessible and will unfold a fiercely coherent masculine core instead of a fragmented, despotic one.

The American Military as Male Initiation

One may consider that the military and the martial career path might be one that could illicit and produce true masculine activation. In America, that is not necessarily so. Militaries historically are machines of social and political agendas. Government would have us believe that armed forces are for the direct protection of a nation under the military threat of another. This implies that an armed military has one sole function: protecting a nation from being completely annihilated by an aggressor.

That kind of threat, however, has occurred only twice in the history of the United States since the Revolutionary War, which were the homeland invasions of the War of 1812 and WWII. The rest of the 20 some odd acts of war or so-called military operations in our brief two-century history have been conducted mostly over political strategies or economic enhancement for domestic capitalist interests abroad. Under false pretenses disguised in what politicians cloak as our "national security interests," war or combat operations have been waged on nations that pose no real threat to this country.

When a military enforces political agenda, it creates, with violence, suitable platforms that serve special interest programs outside of national defense. Institutions that entreat misdirected aggression of this kind do not assist in the cultivation of warriors that naturally evolve into powerful, coherent adult men. This kind of armed force requires soldiers who must live by the Tennyson creed, "theirs is not to reason why, theirs is but to do or die." These are followers, shackled to a chain of command whose orders they cannot afford to question. Allegiance here is simply the soldier to a dimensionless discipline, not necessarily warriors embedded in a noble cause.

Political abstractions regarding wartime agendas will never suffice to illicit full masculine core devotion. Combat, however, is a different story. Pure combat is a distillation of wartime activity that has little to do with the vagaries of the military complex proper. At its heart, combat is a primal, masculine-suited event. Autonomous and self-determining, combat unfolds within a raw field of action that distinguishes itself from the morass of politics and diplomacy.

Military Combat as Initiation

The act of participating in combat requires a great measure of discipline, loyalty, bravery and ferocity on the part of those in the trenches. Ask any male soldier who has experienced significant combat fighting and he will tell you how much the diplomatic necessities of war policy meant to him while he and his platoon of brothers were pinned down in a firefight. Modern soldiers carry out orders without question, and the typical political platforms that shroud and drive wartime agendas have no functional value to them in the heat of battle. Today's modern soldiers accept their duty to serve country with or without a connection to an overarching mission statement that for them is personally inspiring or even ethically justified. The core power of a combat unit's fighting success comes from the fraternal bonds forged within the company of men itself.

It is not necessarily the mandate of the American military to create soldiers who possess heart-confirmed solidarity with the political leaders who sanction the war activity that such soldiers execute. The industrial complex of the military is not ultimately interested in producing totally free and fully realized masculine expression in its soldiers. Political leaders, and to some degree the industrial military complex, do not feel they owe their fighting soldiers the duty of providing a clear and coherent cause worth fighting for. It is a deplorable act of malicious abandonment to sever a young man at war from the heart of what he is fighting for.

Because of the disconnect around the current war in the Middle East, we have instances of post-traumatic stress disorder well in excess of that necessary in times of war. Political leaders who make these kinds of wars without a soul, crafted from ill agendas and saturated in propaganda, dispense a particularly cruel stranglehold upon the human condition. To send a young man to war without an intimate and inspiring connection to his fighting cause is an affront to the heart and soul of a man. How is it we ask a duty-bound young man to kill, and possibly die, for some supposed national threat that has been theorized into being by government officials and politicians? If we want whole men to emerge from our boys, then we had better find true men with impeccable integrity at the highest levels of government to lead them.

It is most assuredly an act of intentional omission to consciously leave out any connection to a culturally necessary exponent of modern warfare from the common soldier. Political leaders like to portray the issues as too complex and nuanced to be of much use to a fighting soldier. That may be true in some respects, but consider even our own Revolutionary War. In that case, no culturally sanctioned connection to the cause of rebellion would have meant that no rural farmers were going to fight some war against mighty England for the vague interests of the colonial landed gentry. In the case of colonial America, the common promise was one of freedom and independence for every white American male from all forms of government tyranny. There was a unifying cause, if it were true, worth fighting for—and against all odds, enough men in that time did.

Because of the political nature of contemporary global warfare, no national military institution would attempt in modern times to gain the hearts and minds of its soldiers and expect to achieve much success, because there is typically no soulful content to modern war actions waged by political leaders. As such, there is nothing there for the soldier's heart to connect to and be inspired by. Such an intimacy would be a prerequisite for a military that supported its soldiers to fully express the masculine core while serving the military, and particularly while they are engaged in conducting combat.

In spite of all this, our boys often perform in the battlefield with heroic proportion, demonstrating masculine core expression rarely achieved in peacetime or in civilian life. However, the feat is summoned from young men whose core instincts press into action an epic masculine performance summoned forth by dire situations. Ideally these combat scenarios should be intimately overseen by elder soldiers in the chain of command who fully grasp the raw totality of the powerfully human event that is happening in the field under their localized command. Training has its value, but the young men who fight the wars with their bodies understand that the heart of a man is what drives all the training into action, not simply the training itself. Ultimately, the common bond of fraternal solidarity is what makes a unit survive in combat.

An Historical Model of Martial Masculine Integration

Ancient Sparta made warriors of their men. We may argue against the desired product of that martial culture, but we may also admire the fact that they directed their boys into men in a very structured and coherent way.

In Sparta, boys understood in no uncertain terms the passage that led to manhood, and the men understood clearly the definition and purpose of a Spartan man's life—the state over the individual, and the individual safeguarding the state.

An allegiance to service beyond oneself is critical to the journey of the authentic male and something Sparta provided for in the rearing of its young men. America, with its free-for-all thematic ethic of "individualism" has unfortunately encouraged an allegiance primarily to one's self. This has brought increasing consequences to an already historically derailed masculine evolution.

Sparta made solid men because it required that masculine commodity for the survival of the Spartan state. Today, corporate interests are the power centers in America and that corporate state, unlike Sparta, requires low-content followers to survive, not real men.

The sources of mass cultural influence and social power today do not provide wisdom for the people. Like any totalitarian regime, contemporary oligarchies abhor the potential collective power of freethinking majorities that thrive in a heart-centered culture. So the money interest organizations divide the people with polarized platforms of nonsense, bombard them with distracting propaganda and dull everyone with empty food and shallow entertainment. The new world oligarchy spawns puppet government leadership and, through that vessel, manipulates the governed masses with fear and distraction. The strategy of money interest power groups is to create a culture of weak, divided and subservient men to feed off of.

If we fail to achieve even what Sparta managed to accomplish, that chiefly being the direct conversion of boys to real men, we remain dangerously lost. For without a wise culture engaging men in some common unifying bond that cultivates an allegiance to some naturally higher principle over individual survival, gain or pleasure, there will be too few real men to draw upon who might challenge the power paradigms and bring about any real change.

Without such men in the future, there will be no redeeming evolution, and I predict, no long-term survival of the species as a whole.

I would offer that today's men have broader options of masculine contribution than that which the warrior mode Spartan culture placed so much emphasis on. I would also suggest that our modern culture demands more from the masculine role than mere martial competency. Though it is essential that we retain our masculine ferocity, contemporary society ought to invite a man to explore the many ways in which the core masculine can express itself potently and coherently by producing a dynamically diverse social landscape of fulfilling opportunities.

6

PAIR BONDING
AND MARRIAGE

She's a rose
The muse in every song
That I can compose.

She's the sun
The victory in every race
That I've run.

— From *The Key*

Pair Bonding
and Marriage

Humans are pair bonders. After adolescence is shed and the young
male is ready to embark on his masculine mission, he will require
the balancing polarity of a female partner and counterpart. While
most ancient marriages were in some way arranged or otherwise culturally preordained, the relatively modern notions of romantically
driven choice selections have supplanted most of the old ways of
facilitating marriage coupling in the west.

In the old standard of arranged marriages you "learned" to love
your husband or wife. Marriage was more a function of tribal cohesion

driven by patriarchal or matriarchal lineages. Marriages like these served to fix class ties, assuring status, wealth and/or harmonious relations between clans. Concerns about romantic fulfillment or the couple's personal compatibility were not primary issues in these types of arrangements.

Modern marriage in the west has adopted dynamics of a romantic courtship designed to lead to an engagement. Individuals in this culture usually seek the right pair bond solely through personal discernment and individual selection. This self-determined method of coupling may be more exciting than an arranged marriage, but it leaves this critical selection process to freshly budding adults with very little life experience and only a dawning sense of themselves as individuals. Though this courtship process is not inferior or wrong, it is a context that contributes to higher divorce rates than those found in the case of arranged marriages.

However, the romance-driven coupling can offer more potential for the husband to experience a deeper surrender to his wife than an arranged marriage might tend to. The leveraging aspect of romance's passion and the capacity of his beloved to personally "stop" him with her beauty invite and encourage an organic masculine surrender to her. The overall surrender to the feminine (that in this case is embodied by a wife) is essential to the masculine core's lifelong journey toward the perfect marriage of surrender and action in the world.

Whatever the method of coupling, whether by luck, grace or by coherent selection, if individuals of integrity do manage to come together to form the right pairing, that bond will display a particular expression that is quite recognizable.

Coherent Coupling

For the masculine part, a coherent union provides a healthy inter-dependence with a woman that sustains him with the foundational radiance of the feminine. The nurturing and the stabilizing presence embodied in the feminine allows him to cantilever his activation out into the world potently. Because of her influence, his natural capacity for power and force in the world will now be extended exponentially and with greater effect and vitality. Under her influence, the masculine will achieve more, endure more and rejuvenate faster. She affirms and quickens his masculine potential and agenda. The effect is profound and can literally transform a mediocre man into one capable of heroic proportions.

His capacity as a young man to relate to and engage her feminine core will dictate directly his ability to manifest his own masculine power potential. The more he can surrender to her coherent feminine essence, the deeper will be the experience of his own masculine current, preparing him for the essential descent into ashes beginning in middle age. This relational union will, through time, strengthen his ability to continually sublimate his actions in the world through the blessings and affirmation of the feminine. In the long term, the practice will provide a middle-aged man the requisite experience to fully engage the coming midlife deconstruction of his entire subjective reality.

For the feminine part, the union provides a healthy interdependence that will, among other things, provide healthy masculine modeling for her children. The pairing also fosters for her security, protection, direction and material sustenance. Her core expression in the world will be honored, nurtured and celebrated to ensure that it may flourish. Her masculine consort will champion her feminine cause and provide for her a modicum of protection and relief from environmental assaults or human molestations. He will also serve as a grounding influence to his beloved's wild and unqualified feminine expression, much to her appreciation and relief.

Such a man will strive to bring shelter to her from all unnecessary tension and fatigue. The sustaining of her core radiance represents his first line of service in the world, never failing to neglect it for anything else the world can offer, for he understands the treasure he protects is the very nectar and nucleus that energizes his days.

A marriage coupling rooted in this quality of expression will flourish for life if the bond is meant to last that long. If the pairing is not a lifetime contract, in spite of the fact that there are the elements of a coherent masculine/feminine partnership, the two souls will likely separate in time for other reasons and move on. They will probably remain deep friends for life, recognizing and honoring the residual coherency that initiated and served their union during its time.

The Dance

A true masculine/feminine coupling cannot be fundamentally compartmentalized into separate spheres of actualization in an attempt to simply pronounce one as the manifesting doer and the other as the activating principle. The very act of coherent polarity coupling in truth creates a circle of expression where it merely appears that one is an acting agent and the other a passive one.

These apparent roles sublimate the very moment a true coupling consecrates each heart to the other. For even though each person will emphasize the expression of a masculine/feminine agent in the partnership, the alchemy of the coupling will weave together all of the male-female elements into a whole new tapestry, one that is in such a state of expressive flux that it can no longer really claim such archetypal gender distinctions as being solely attributable to one or the other, any more than the mouth of a river emptying into the sea can delineate the absolute line where sea water begins and fresh water ends.

It can be said that in the dance of roles, the feminine nurtures, inspires, energizes and counsels the masculine, while the masculine actualizes his essence while serving the feminine that sustains him. But truly, where can the line of separation be drawn in such a coupling? Where may we find such a clear distinction of cause and effect between the masculine and feminine when the two conspire to bring forth, from the source of creation itself, expression into the world?

In fact it is here that the gender archetypes merge to transcend gender role archetypes as a matter of pure expression emanating forth from the pairing. It is impossible to say who is giving and who is receiving in such a bond.

Organic Fidelity

Truly bonded couples are no longer moving singularly. The temptation to unilaterally move outside of the circle of intimacy of such a coupling does not arise because the act, or even the very notion of infidelity, is not congruent with the living sense of solidarity and accord that is expressed in the relationship. So the action of monogamy in this case comes not from the typical moral bolstering, but proceeds organically, naturally unfolding out of a sense of profound consensual unity that has been well-established by a grace-endowed rapport that the couple co-creates, moment to moment.

I qualify with the words "grace-endowed" because this kind of bond cannot be forged without being first ordained by life itself. That's the mystery and power of it. As a couple, if you recognize that and surrender to it, you dance in the magic of it all your days together. Nothing external can compromise these kinds of sanctified pair bonds.

Marriage vows exclaim promises of fidelity. But no vow, no matter how passionately expressed, can completely withstand the sheer scope and magnitude of life's complex and unrelenting assault on the static doctrines of men. True monogamy is discovered only through dynamic surrender to the fluid love you embrace with your beloved. The practice of living through a deeply bonded union prepares a man for the midlife transition he will make in the deconstruction phase. His active and ongoing surrender to the coherent coupling of his marriage will complement his efforts as he descends into the interior mystery of his own being.

Unconscious Relationships

Unfortunately, what more often occurs with marital unions in actual life is the unconscious marriage. Here two people simply act out acquired roles that on the surface can vaguely appear like a functional partnership.

What is actually occurring in these cases is a co-dependent standoff, a veritable "cease-fire" of true impulses. These couplings become a mutually unrealized emotional and psychic enmeshment that hunkers down for the long haul. Blanketed in a kind of muted desperation, these relationships careen through the years hoping at best not to hit a landmine event (such as an affair) that will rupture irreparably the fragile dysfunction that loosely holds the coupling together. Whether partnerships of this nature may hold together for a long or short time no one can be certain, but what is certain is that that they are not held together properly.

The masculine version of this distorted contract trades in the sacred expressions of the masculine archetype for the dark errors of the unconscious man.

For men, unconscious relationship with another begins with an unconscious relationship with self. Un-integrated masculine expression has very little forward sense. Interrelational sensibilities such as empathy, compassion, toleration, tenderness and nurturing are typically somewhere approaching vacant in such men. Due to the absence of core male grounding, the generally proactive qualities such as boldness, vision and initiative are also lacking.

Men in these states do little more than what is pressingly required of them. As a result, an entire culture of crisis management protocol has become unconsciously indoctrinated into our social functioning. How many people must get killed at an intersection before they install a stop light signal? How many people must get sick and die in one area before we stop a nearby manufacturing facility from polluting the groundwater?

Because men are not awake unto themselves, they are in a kind of passive sleepwalk, running on the fumes of their closed-in personal paradigm. It is as if they are breathing in their own psychic exhalation over and over again—nothing fresh, revitalizing or inspirational enters the system.

Where there could be healthy interdependence in a pair bond there is now a perilous codependent tension. The genuine adoration of her total beauty is replaced by a morose scrutiny of her physical wasting due to the parasitic leaching of her feminine vitality by the husband.

Where there could be protection, there is now a stifling control. Where there could be the support and recognition of her radiant core, there is now exploitation and depletion of that feminine fountainhead.

Where there could be selfless masculine service, there is now a self-centered, particularly male pathology. Where there could be benevolent masculine leadership and direction, there is now only violent uncertainty and self-doubt.

Within a couple of decades of living out this dysfunctional existence, the derailed masculine agent may be reduced to a brooding morass of dark volatility with years of misdirected momentum behind it. He is lost and dangerous at this stage of his journey, ripe mostly for cheap coping strategies that distract, but do not serve life. In a marriage this may reveal itself as an extramarital affair or some other midlife crisis fix.

Mediating marital crises situated exactly in these conditions often reveals a repeating theme where women have had enough. Men in these kinds of cases are stunned to face the actuality of losing the object of support they have for so many years depended on. As the marriage moves into the death zone, the wife will often consolidate her strength, coalescing her consecration to finally live her life without him if need be.

As he begins to feel the full impact of the loss of the radiance that had sustained his false masculine for so long, all that is left for him is a horrifying sense of emptiness and powerlessness that reflects years of true masculine core dismissal and neglect.

He is now faced with a critical choice: confront his own lie and seek redemption or deepen the denial that allowed the original error to exist. It does not matter how, or to what degree, a man experiences this midlife passage circumstantially; as a man he will encounter it at some point in his life. At that threshold the only answer to that moment will be found in the radical descent into himself—the full-scale transmutation of the midlife deconstruction.

DECONSTRUCTION

Pulverize this grainy meal
Beneath your ever turning wheel
Till powder blown away reveals
What birth and death
Could never steal.
— From *Grist*

Deep Surrender

At some point in a man's life, his service to wife, children, family, community and the earth will no longer suffice to provide an absolute sense of complete functioning that fulfills him completely. There will come a time when that individual must be drawn inward, to the depths of his own being, where the fundamental relationship between himself and life will finally be reconciled. His life of service nobly directed toward external subjects outside himself has only been a practice run, relative to the complete and utter surrender he will now make before the altar of life and the entity that created him.

A man must at some point offer up everything to the Living Intelligence that waits for the prodigal son to return home. Call it what you will—God, The Divine, The Creator, Great Mystery, Higher

95

Power, it doesn't matter. What is essential is that a man ultimately submits his personal will to the service of the One Great Living Intelligence that gives rise to all things. Out of this act will come the resurrection of a new order of full masculine activation and expression.

Due to the lack of a coherent social structure it is exceedingly rare that a man will consciously and successfully surrender his personal will in his adult years, choosing to do so of his own volition or without provocation. For most men in the culture this act of surrender will occur on the heels of the intense suffering that builds over a lifetime of relatively unconscious, self-centered activity and culminates in what I refer to as a threshold event. Threshold events often follow an intense calamity of circumstances that forces the individual to completely confront his personal paradigm and his life process. Moving through to the other side of such an ordeal properly will produce a surrendered and wholly integrated man. If a man at the threshold stage refuses to descend and surrender into the depths of his own disillusionment, he will stumble forth from the occasion broken and driven deeper into a brooding fragmentation. He may never again have such a profound opportunity to realize the sublime connection to all of life that the midlife deconstruction is designed to reveal.

Women typically get elements of this surrender to life, organically integrated, through the experiences of menses and child-bearing. Men however have no such somatic instruction to draw upon, and therefore must initiate the requisite experiences to catalyze their perceptive awareness into a living understanding. If men do not initiate through their own volition or through cultural ceremony designed to promote this rite of passage, it will be thrust upon them harshly by a life equation that seeks balance, harmony and coherency of expression.

The surrender is essential, for it provides an integration of elements crucial to a full and coherent masculine life expression. A sense of connection to all life must now be wedded to the masculine core, with an understanding that it cannot be controlled, only experienced—only lived. In tandem with this almost mystical sense of universal interconnectivity comes a deepening release of the personal will into the current of Universal Intelligence. Without these elements of connection and subjective release of personal will fully integrated into the masculine core, male activity cannot express itself without residuals of some form of violence attached.

Adult Male Midlife Deconstruction

Eventually the dream of the subjective self that in youth was so passionately constructed as ego experiences a gradual breakdown by degree and at midlife stages is now reaching the point of no return, hovering on the brink of total dissolution. This radical phase is necessary for the next stage of a man's life, and often comes in the form of the ever-clichéd midlife crisis.

In midlife the subjective instrument of the personal self has become heavy-laden, saturated with the experiences of life, at a time when the physical body is beginning to wane from the zenith of its youthful potency. When this boulevard of broken dreams mutates into the life crisis that will precipitate the threshold event, the invitation to the midlife deconstruction passage begins.

At midlife deconstruction, the nature and quality of the transition is profoundly different from the adolescent passage. Midlife surrender comes in the form of the total deconstruction of the subjective personal self, whereas the youthful passage was focused primarily on the construction of it.

This transformation is markedly unlike the transitional movement in adolescence where the freshly formed ego reifies its newfound subjective posture by utilizing its individuated power and force in action. In those early stages of a male's evolution, the emphasis is on personal power in the face of death. For men later on in life it becomes all about the death of the personal paradigm in the face of life.

For American men, the disillusionment that comes hard on the heels of core mid-passage life ruptures will reveal cultural promises and social contracts that have sold them an artificial bill of goods from the beginning. It often becomes excruciatingly clear to a man at this stage of his life that from the time he was first indoctrinated into this social system, he was buying into a society that fundamentally had no core wisdom governing it. There becomes embedded in the masculine psyche a sense of betrayal, and the corresponding sense of lost investment and confusion feels staggering.

For men caught in this disillusionment there is no longer a clear bearing. There is no certain tack to hold to anymore and it seems at once that all the rules have changed. This event is no mere funk, depression or stress-induced breakdown such as the vicissitudes of the past.

For the man who has attempted to physically reify his potency through external validations in an attempt to assuage the edge of his midlife anxiety, the game is over. This time in his life is calling for something much more profound then external validation. The movement at this time must be about inward reorganization, and not outward reanimation. A man has reached the stage in his life where the subjective psychic identity must end its reign and finally sublimate into the singularity of the Godhead.

This window of opportunity must not be squandered in the desperate attempt of trying to restructure some sophomoric psychic posture of male potency. The opening is an essential occasion of critical import that must be boldly pierced to enter the requisite descent into the ashes.

This stage is an agonizing one that typically only a minority of men will choose to meet fully. This phase of male life will completely break a man if he is strong enough to allow it to. Submitting to this deconstruction fully will allow him to discover what remains after the shattering of all things personal and subjective in his world. If he succeeds he will have found the pearl of great price, which is his core being and upon that rock he will build a true man, the final mainfestation of himself that he will live out the rest of his days with.

For such men, the time is at hand for the absolute and total razing of the personal self. The level, depth and scope of utter surrender that is required of men at this juncture of their lives must be fully engaged. The total subjective identity of the personal self must burn to the ground, for out of the ashes will arise the phoenix of the liberated masculine core.

The following is an unedited entry from my journal during my own midlife breakdown that occurred in my 39th year:

> I want to reach down inside myself and find something there. Something that gives me life, and a will to live it. But I feel nothing right now but emptiness and confusion. It's like I cannot get deeper than this feeling that my life has been a strategy to survive and nothing much more. It's as if anything worth valuing in my lifetime of expression came only on the heels of my perceived safety in it. I am tired of plotting and planning.

Tired of trying to find a way to thrive. Tired of trying to love and wondering if it is first and foremost the grasping of a fearful human being, scared of facing this emptiness alone. Tired of trying to ensure that an escape route for my tentative existence is always available. Tired of trying to face this train wreck of human affairs with hope and conviction. I question whether I want to survive anymore at all, even whether I want to keep peeling off of life's breast some share of milk to prevent me from feeling hunger and weakness. I wonder at my life's moments of laughter and accomplishment, whether I was merely full of myself and drunk with pride the whole time. I wonder if there was really even one sincere breath of life I have actually taken into this body clear of any agenda to win or succeed. Maybe it was all a sham, since the first moment I realized I was truly alone. Maybe all my living and loving has been a rage against the biting feeling of being alone and vulnerable. Maybe I have merely stepped on everyone and everything I thought I loved in this life, just to keep my own head above water. Maybe I'm a deal maker, not a lover. Maybe I hate myself for this shadow that follows me everywhere, this dark mirror that reminds me of my polished hypocrisy. Maybe every gift I have ever been given has been squandered on self-preservation, like a king who lives in luxury off the sweat of his own people. Maybe I am a liar beyond repair. A hopeless user of life.

As this entry demonstrates, nothing short of the complete dismantling of the personal paradigm of the individual self will heal the sting that reality brings to a man in the midst of such darkness.

Again, surrender here is not mere resignation or some form of indifferent disregard. It is the absolute surrender to the Heart of Life we learn about of Christ on the cross. It is the most passionate of acts, demonstrating the total acquiescence of the personal self to the ultimate will of the Creator.

In fact, Christ's crucifixion was a landmark event in human conscious evolution of the masculine core. It marks one of the rare instances that a man chose to consciously and fully surrender his personal will to the will of the Creator without the prompting of a forced calamity, at the astoundingly youthful age of his early thirties.

Christ surrendered his life fully in the zenith of his youthful bloom, an exceedingly rare accomplishment, and one that has had profound residual effects on human evolution ever since. The Christ phenomenon allowed the typical age of descent integration to occur in the earlier stages of a man's life, so that a fully coherent masculine core expression could be realized far sooner than it had typically been actualized before.

Yet, even given Christ's powerful example, very few men will approach this transition voluntarily before calamity-level suffering prompts it. Still, it is exciting and encouraging that we have Christ and the Buddha as two legendary examples of an early-aged voluntary descent into ashes, integrating a relatively youthful deconstruction passage of the masculine archetype well before the imminent approach of middle or old age.

Most men will organically surrender to life in a gradual way as they age, and the decline of the body slowly invites an acceptance of surrender as the death door approaches. As men begin to embrace deconstruction in these ripening years they will become full with the archetypal wisdom of elders who achieve this deepening milestone.

The Threshold Event

It takes decades of living to amass a subjective empire that has the capacity to energize a quality of surrender that is worthy of an apotheosis-level act, and that is why deconstruction usually strikes the middle-aged man.

Typical adult male midlife deconstruction comes on the heels of what I have referred to as the threshold event. This is a marker life disruption, often occurring in midlife, when the somatic cycles are calling for radical transformation that no mild adjustment or modest modification of current operating systems can satisfy.

Threshold events tend to trigger a personal breakdown because there is the initial realization that one is operating from a subjective paradigm that is no longer sufficient to perpetuate the self through any sort of appropriately meaningful existence.

The coping mechanisms of escape through substance abuse, sex, power or obsession with career no longer work. The status quo of the personal self has become intolerable for some deeply seated unknown reason, and the cutting sense of it can no longer be dismissed or ignored. Everywhere men in these conditions look, there is nothing apparent to them that will soothe the raw discontent they are experiencing.

Threshold events can take the form of a critical accumulation of stressful circumstances that culminate, or a more striking rupture such as a health, career, financial or marital crisis, or even the death of a loved one. Whatever form the circumstance takes, it will serve to suddenly shatter the constancy of the personally created "safe and stable" psychic environment that the individual has operated within his whole life. In my work, many men have arrived there through the threshold event of either criminal incarceration or divorce.

Men who find themselves in this situation have a window of opportunity to right their course, and it is essential that they seize the moment. It takes too much vitality to square off to these dark psychic gauntlets later on in life, and once you turn away from the self-work that you know now needs to be done at these critical junctures, you may never get a second opportunity to deconstruct that deeply again.

To qualify as a threshold event, a circumstance must be significant enough in scope and effect that what it stimulates in the individual is not consolable when employing any of the individual's prior life-coping strategies. There is nothing currently in the individual's psychic toolbox that will enable him to cope with or "handle" the current emotional and psychic rift.

This is the magic and power of the threshold event; it is unmanageable when confronted solely from the context of the limitations inherent in the existing subjective paradigm. The profound lack of a sense of control and powerlessness that the threshold event distills will serve to leverage the deep surrender that will invite the space for grace to bestow the needed whole-scale change.

It is essential that a man have it in him to move through this life passage without contraction during this crucial conversion phase. For if he accepts the full weight and measure of the revealed confusion, disorientation and utter sense of powerlessness that result from having stripped back the veil of his own grand disillusionment, he will receive the gift of being driven by grace deep into the heart of the clear masculine core.

If he can do all this, without bargaining for less than the full scope of disorientation and uncertainty that this initiation will bring, he will then experience directly the resurrection of his male potency exponentially enhanced, and now be wisely guided and directed by an Intelligence larger than himself.

This midlife passage calling for the subjugation of the personal paradigm is not designed to be conducted within the crucible of any structured ritual form. It is a wholly unscripted event, initiated and executed by grace, and each man will be called upon to drag his own particular cross to Golgotha.

During the deconstruction following the threshold event, no program can prepare him, no person can guide or console him, and no medicine can relieve him from the absolute breakdown of the personal self.

The Descent into Ashes

The often grotesque and mind-shattering process of male psychic deconstruction is no place for the meek or mild. To descend into the shadows and groundless abyss of the human condition requires a quality that falls somewhere between total abandon and absolute integrity. To meet the bloated demons that wait inside our internal personal structure will require truly heroic qualities.

That journey is reflected classically in the famous story of the heroic "Geat" Beowulf, who goes to meet Grendel, the terrible monster who devours the greatest of Dane warriors. Grendel's terrifying power rests in his acumen for exploiting masculine error. Over and over he lays waste to men who cannot fully surrender to their own truth, and so instinctively, Beowulf awaits Grendel without armor, without weapon.

Beowulf metaphorically waits to confront the beast naked because he knows that the battle with Grendel will not be about any conventional combat. The battle with Grendel takes place within the tortured landscape of our own masculine psyche. For Grendel is not just the horrific monster proper, he is an amalgam of all our deepest psychic terrors and aversions. Engaging our own personal Grendel means embracing what amounts to an extension of every dark corner of our traumatized psyches. Grendel strikes terror into the hearts of men because he is borne of the fertile and terrified imagination of mankind itself.

The depth of our repulsion to Grendel arises from our own wretched inner emptiness. The more we avoid him, the less we see how Grendel is really born of the seed of our own darkness. And if we ultimately fail to confront him, the space between the beast and ourselves will one day disappear, and in that act of careless fusion he will ultimately devour us.

Most young men keep a mistress of false pretense or clever denial all through their youthful years. That has to change at some point, because those kinds of operators will fall victim to Grendel's appetite for half-men. It is ironic, but Grendel demands a deeper relationship to life and to oneself. He is the dark chalice from which we must all finally drink, and he is as necessary to the lost soul as the Holy Grail was to the Knights of the Round Table.

Ultimately we must come to finally embrace Grendel for what he is, the stunted offspring of our half-lived lives, he who bears the measured counterweight to all of our folly-filled days in the sun.

The ultimate paradox is that Grendel cannot be destroyed. He cannot be pursued. He must be reconciled, so that he learns his place in the face of the heroic heart. Christ utters, "Satan, get thee behind me" and the full masculine core arises, sending the beast in agony loping back to his lair in the shadows. The beast is not to be slain, he is to be mastered.

Those who do choose to confront Grendel will find that the outcome of this engagement will produce no real victor because the fruits of that contest transcend both opponents. Reconciling Grendel will manifest a new order of core power that will finally bring to an end all remaining residue of masculine error, and make a fully realized man out of a merely well-intentioned one.

For the sake of our own redemption, Grendel must be subsumed by the nakedly heroic silence at the center of our being. Our soul will then find redemption against the fallen state Grendel embodies so that we may finally arise and, like Beowulf, be men among boys.

Not This, Not This

Deconstructing the subjective self is not an action one takes with a goal toward a dissolution of the egoistic-self. This has been a misguided aspect of some so-called spiritual endeavors for quite some time. The call to the negation of the subjective ego toward idealized notions of nirvana, attainment, liberation or enlightenment are circle paths to nowhere. What I am referring to is a movement that will establish and cultivate a conscious integration of the objective impersonal self so that it can witness the subjective functioning of the personal mechanism as an agent of service to the will of the Creator.

We must ultimately reconcile these two distinct natures within the human condition. Whether we label these natures the personal versus the impersonal, the sacred versus the profane, the conscious versus the unconscious, the purely mortal versus the Divine, the ignorant versus the wise, the heart versus the head, the soul versus the ego or the dreaming versus the awakened, the theme is ever the same. One nature needs to submit and reconcile to the other. Though this endeavor is not commonly achieved today, it is essential that we as humans embody this artful living in order to facilitate the next evolution.

The first movement for men on this journey toward deconstructive transformation is identifying all static perceptions and closed-circuit paradigms of the isolated subjective self that are causing the bulk of resistance toward a core surrender to the impersonal dimension of being. These psychic constructs misdirect vast amounts of attention toward non sequitur ends, and deplete precious vital energy within the system of conscious awareness. Within the rising tide of fluid transformation, we must break down the mind's psychic carnivals because it is essential that they no longer continue to function as the sole proprietor of presence within the open field of embodied conscious awareness.

Sorting through the morass of perceptive error at the onset of deconstruction will seem initially, to the subject, to be a morbid and overwhelming task, and in a very real sense it can be. But the goal is not to necessarily rid the subjective presence of all its misguided psychic debris.

The typical process, and the one that occurred in my case, reflects more of a gradual diminishment of the grip of the subjective paradigm over general consciousness until the balance of the personal self begins to give way to the growing sense of the ineffable and impersonal presence at the un-center of our being. The equation of the new balance of consciousness unfolding at this stage of deconstruction, in retrospect, seems almost mathematical in function and execution, but the details deserve a more specific elucidation.

The Awareness Equation

As the process unfolds, an objective relationship with the dramatic and reactive paradigms of the self-identifying persona will begin to release the hold that the personal lens has on the general field of quantum awareness we have access to. This release will begin to ease the resistances of the personal self and its associated habitual reactions, while holding space for other possibilities and understandings to arise from within the larger field of ephemeral intelligence.

This evolution creates a relaxation and spaciousness that the individual experiences beyond the narrow features of the old habituated stimulus-response protocols. This new marked ability to access and respond from the expansive core masculine begins to precipitate a claim of functional sovereignty over subjective presence by the impersonal field of awareness.

Men will often report a sense of "relief" as they relax into this new core stability, instead of solely expressing themselves from the complex and often trauma-distorted processes of the limited subjective field of neurological functioning they had been captives to prior to the new expansive awakening. With the newfound spaciousness in awareness and action, the subject may now begin to access and "hear" the Universal Intelligence that creates and governs all life through the field of impersonal awareness, without undue distortion from the typically static judgments and inaccurate perceptions of the personal self.

The residual entropy within the overall system of individual awareness now begins to reveal itself to the enlightened mind's scrutiny, and the light of that discerning presence begins to alter and diminish the overall influence of the interloping error. The clearing field of awareness carries with it an accommodation of integrity that begins to note the relationship between an individual's potential expression and the one he is actualizing moment to moment. If the measure of his action in the world is not commensurate with the measure of his coherent potential, he will find that a troubling sense of profound hypocrisy will settle in. If the movement is destined toward evolution, then an algorithmic alchemy will undo the entropic influence by degree in the face of the liberated awareness field. In due course the error will finally fade into obscurity because it is no longer being energized with Presence.

Being immersed in this larger sublime Presence facilitates a new broader posturing of awareness that allows for a man to access and express deeper wisdom, sourced from a pool of The Living Intelligence beyond the reach of the brain's closed knowledge base.

So it is that men who accomplish this transformation exhibit a particular power and authority in their actions uncommon to the general cross section of male activation. The potent Presence of such men is noticed in any room they enter, and the residue of their influence is experienced long after they leave.

The authority such men exude is derived from action rooted in the impersonal, heart-centered primacy of the human operating potential. The Presence of such men is unmistakably fluid, clear, certain and bold. Sourcing from benevolent insight, inspiration and intuition, the activation of such men is potent and unaffected by negative karma residues, within or without their personal sphere. This fully coherent masculine expression is often seen as graceful and clear in its discernment and confident and inexorable in its execution.

Negotiating the new terrain of relating to and with the subjective self, (rather than being fused with it), while anchored in the referential wisdom of the impersonal awareness field, will for such realized men now be the new operating order of being in the world.

Tapping the Core

The core of the masculine is discovered as the residual content of Presence remaining after the process of deconstruction of the personal subjective paradigm has factored in. I mean deconstruction in the sense that men no longer "live" solely out of the psychic structures that were present, not necessarily that those structures no longer exist. In the new order of functioning, a man now finds a "relationship" with his own subjective model. Now there is a spaciousness between his conceptual paradigm and the choice of action he will undertake in any given moment. The individual is no longer fused to the framework of his own limited reality, and the space in between allows for a greater Intelligence to direct a more coherent choice of response to the moment at hand.

However, the whole process when first encountered can be disturbingly sublime upon the initial integration. Men in particular have difficulty grounding into a core sense of Intelligence that they cannot locate in time or space, or that they cannot personally manipulate or willfully control. The act requires an unfamiliar exercise in surrender. But once the sense of this fluid way of being is felt and recognized at length, the actualization of the new masculine expression emerges more and more as the individual utilizes the subtle nature of the core self as a referential touchstone for wholeness in action. This in fact is the gift of having integrated the feminine prior to deconstruction.

The sublime nature of the true masculine core is the singular most difficult thing for men to reconcile on the journey toward authentic masculine expression. The "hard" identity of the subjective self had heretofore provided a smoke-and-mirrors version of self-identity that for many decades had sufficed as "real." However upon total deconstruction of the personal self, the old "identity-device" is revealed to be of zero content, and men are plunged into the core of themselves without bearing. Moving through the event will require the embracing of the missing link of feminine power; the inevitability of total surrender.

The Singularity of Intimacy

The singularity of intimacy is the essential journey of aloneness a man must make toward the zenith of that individual's sense of separateness as a created entity. There the threshold of his singular expression will pierce the veil of mystery and dissolve into the unknown, and a new order of sublime relationship to life itself will be established that forever supplants the prior struggling sense of self as a separate isolated creature.

The radical process of transmutation that occurs in the lives of post-deconstruction men will have profound affects on all of their external relationships. Oftentimes the community of old friends and relations will no longer relate to a man's new way of functioning in life. The need for a new order of true and authentically meaningful relationships will begin to discern and select for meaningful exchanges, and many of the older established bonds that were built on the old relational dynamic will simply cease to continue. In fact, many of the former friends and family members may begin to turn on the new man they see.

The situation may be compared to a stage play where the actor suddenly stops the play on stage and steps out of character. The audience, which came to be entertained, will not take kindly to this sudden intrusion of realism into the drama it has significantly invested in. A man who is radically unfolding a new masculine wholeness from the whole-scale deconstruction and reintegration of the personal self had better be prepared for the wrath of those who do not like reality in their fiction.

In fact, a man is not prepared for a full-scale integration of the deconstruction passage if he requires some dimension of support from others to sustain his core ability to act boldly through the process. Men who are inappropriately dependent upon a spiritual teacher, a lover or a community of friends engage in a collusion that will only serve to insulate them from the raw experience of a solitary conscious transmutation. This primacy of aloneness precipitates the singularity of intimacy that is a portal not unlike death itself, where no two incarnated individuals can go together.

It is essential to remind men that a woman cannot accompany a man into the naked heart of his own existence at deconstruction. A common mistake made by well-intentioned men is to enlist the aid of a beloved woman in accompanying him to the point of his soul's singularity. The singularity of intimacy is not meant to be approached by partnership, and to attempt to do so is simply the spawn of a well-intentioned, but co-dependent residue. Lancelot fell victim to this mechanism of error and by distraction and depletion he never reached the Holy Grail because the intimacy of singularity does not accept couples.

Men who are not willing to absolutely fall off the edge of their conceptual reality and allow themselves to surrender and dissolve into the mystical realm of the unknowable void will make this kind of miscue. There are no back doors, no handholds, no safety nets, no second chances, no one else and no going back at the event horizon of singularity awareness integration.

The perpetuation of the conceptual illusion of one's own self as a primary reality will not survive the process of deconstruction. No one really dies, but no one emerges the same as the way he went in, and that's the paradox you are required to reconcile when you surrender completely. If you have it in you to fulfill the ultimate potential of this essential component of the masculine mission, you will commit to apprehending the singularity of intimacy with a pure heart, a feat fulfilled by the legendarily potent souls represented in the Galahad Heart, the Christ Consciousness and the Buddha Nature.

Fortunately today, the accomplishment, no longer the reserve of the heroic few, has now become the birthright of our species, and the time is at hand to unfold that potential as men, exponentially.

The Realized Man as Leader, Guide and Mentor

After a man has successfully achieved intimacy with his full masculine core, his authority becomes palpable to everyone, and particularly to the young men who encounter such a presence. The feel and sense of that core masculine field will inspire younger men to rally around the cause of their elder brother.

For young men there is an undercurrent of psychic transmission that is occurring while engaged in fraternal interaction to such established men. For the young men, a subtle seed of discontent is being sown deep within their hearts as they fill the draft behind the wake of powerful older men. The potent example of radical authenticity displayed by their fully realized elder brother is, by osmosis, initiating a necessary rift within their young psychic structure. These young men are feeling the dawning sense of unrealized potential in their own lives contrasting with that of the fully realized masculine core of the elder brother they observe. The lure of their own journey, fueled by a passionate self-integrity toward their own full potential as men in the world, is awakening.

It is essential that, for young men, there are available living embodiments of actualized males to bond with and learn from. One of the most important functions of fully coherent men is to model by example a life of integrity to which the young will by nature respond to. Without such guides, mentors and leaders demonstrating coherent masculine wisdom, we will continue to lose our young men to the false gods of cultural hype.

For the post-deconstruction realized man, his actions will continue as an active leader among men serving his culture until he feels within himself a waning capacity for action that exhibits a significant diminishment of his contemporary relevance, coupled with a compelling draw toward the passage into the shaman years.

Shaman Years

The service of the shamanic male elder recedes into the realm of the subtler aspects of existence as the end of his life approaches, allowing for the organic sublimation of his previously piercing subjective presence into the ineffable. His choices are governed now by the influence of the fluid mystical now fully surrounding his life and infusing his awareness. Immersed in the encompassing sense of the impending abyss of death's door approaching, his rationale becomes tempered by his deepening surrender to the inevitability of the vast unknown he will soon dissolve into.

The masculine core of the shamanic male elder no longer distinguishes between the known and the unknown realms. He straddles the worlds of heaven and earth, and the dramas of the human condition carry little import for him now, much in the same way that the colors of a sunset by degree fade as the sun dips below the horizon, yielding inevitably to the black of the evening sky. His relevance as a man exists now in the powerful medicine of his elder stage. He simultaneously holds the hand of God and of his children at the same time, becoming a conduit to the mystical realm for the active generations.

What the shamanic elder offers is a pure and unperturbed vision of masculine action that is absolutely free of the residues of subjective collusion. He points toward a dedicated vision of transcendent expression, inviting the younger men who can intuit it to rise to the occasion. Without the influence of the shamanic male elder, the balance of male actualization in the world would not evolve. Active men can neither build from previous generations of success nor learn from a previous generation's errors without the testimony of the elder wisdom. Without the transmissions of the fiercely sublime shaman presence, history, as they say, will repeat itself.

Death of the Father

The psychic, emotional and hereditary link that exists between father and son is written in an invisible ink that most men cannot read until they lose their father to death. No man can be prepared for what presents itself to the psyche and emotional body when the father dies. No matter whether your father was good or bad, loved or loathed, present or absent, as a son, the legacy of your bond to him is inescapable.

Most men find themselves in the midlife stage when their fathers pass. When my father pierced the veil, I found myself in my mid-40s and a few years down the road past my deconstruction passage. Even though I was grounded in my core, when my father died I felt thrust forward into life's headwinds in a way I had never known before. I realized I had been, in the most archetypal way, drafting off of my father's generational lead. It took me by complete surprise to sense this raw feeling of being the absolute leading edge of my own existence.

My father is now with the ancestors, and like all fathers before him, his living legacy lives on inside his son. The man who showed me how to negotiate life as best he could now has made a passage through death that one day I too will make, and like so many other things in my life before, my father has gone there ahead of me.

The loss of the father is the loss of the sheath that has for so long set around the sword of the son. After a man's father passes, the son's blade can no longer be merely a utensil of his hidden potential; it now must be the absolute edge of his life's work in the world. A fully realized man will never again put away the instrument of his cutting power in the world once the death of the father has come to pass.

For a coherently realized man, the death of his father will quicken the spirit of the son's masculine core and catapult it into the zenith of its activation in the world. He will burn brightly until his life's work is fulfilled, and then the passive call to the shaman years will beckon him off the stage of human drama, out of the spotlight and into the wings where he will whisper influences to younger men from the shadow regions of the ancestors.

THE RESPONSIBILITY
OF THE MASCULINE

For who does claim this scarred remain
So haunting and so bleak
That makes it seem
What happened here
Unnatural and freak?

— From *Monuments, Monoliths,*
Pyramids and Men

Stewardship of Nature

Men ought to be the caretakers of the natural world that sustains them. It is the natural order of the feminine to bring forth abundance without provocation or invocation. What is required by men is a wise stewardship and a considerate care of the natural world before harvesting the sustaining abundance it offers. Yet sacred masculine stewardship of the feminine is a process that can so easily devolve into something profane and violent. There is a clear line that exists between responsible, coherent masculine care and abusive, controlling male violence.

Agricultural endeavors can so easily reduce themselves to a toxic and homogeneous assault on the land and water. Respecting the dignity and diversity of nature means honoring its unmanipulated organic functioning. If men must impose engineered landscapes, they ought to consider the natural order in their design so as not to unwisely scar and blight a normally balanced and healthy environment.

Animal husbandry can so easily turn into neglect and abuse of domesticated creatures. The humane and dignified care of domestic animals ought to be as important as any profits, use or pleasure derived from them.

The conscious and respectful hunting and killing of an animal for food by humans ought to be as natural and coherent an act for men as it is in the animal kingdom between prey and predator. Human beings hunting food for survival is an ancient and direct experience of life consuming life to live. Yet hunting wild game for food can so easily devolve into trophy-sport entertainment, a killing that represents no regard for the sanctity of the taking of animal life.

Perhaps the deepest violation of proper male stewardship, because of the sheer scope and scale, is the unconscious procuring of store-bought meat by the masses of humanity that give little to no consideration of how the animal that provided that packaged meat was treated. Did that animal's quality of life suffer under domestic conditions of cruelty, abuse, neglect or indifference to its dignity as a living creature? There is only peripheral discussion about the consciousness and conditions around the slaughtering of the animal meat we consume. The passivity and indifference regarding these issues is a masculine omission of duty and care.

In the end, it is not the domestication or taking of a life that defines violence, it is the consciousness and coherent necessity around the execution of it that determines whether the act is sacred or profane. A proper masculine stewardship of the feminine dictates an alignment of conscience and action that transcends the heart-numbing habits of our forefathers whose actions were more often derived from achieving economic bottom lines. We as men are responsible for how we move and act on the planet, and when our actions serve to dignify the creation we inhabit, rather than to exploit it, we will find a sense of meaning and fulfillment few of our forefathers ever knew.

Feminine Radiance

A culture is only as good as it treats its women. Whether that statement invokes indictment or celebration in reference to any particular culture speaks volumes about what is happening in terms of the masculine expression there. Much in the same way that men live upon the face of the earth, they move in relation to women. Depletion, exploitation, pollution and control are dark aspects of toxic male conduct mirrored in the treatment of both our environment and our women.

Under the veneer of most women in America today is an exhausted female. More often than not her core radiance has been shattered and drained because men do not understand how to replenish it by caring for the open and abundant vitality she so naturally wants to offer. Unrealized men will often take from a woman's reserves of nurturance and radiance and give little in return. Women in these circumstances are exhausted, feeling empty inside, scared and overwhelmed. Like the burdened environment, they suffer quietly and endure the load, but underneath, the fragility and despair they feel erodes their core radiance.

Here in America women have been cultured to keep quiet and be "good girls." They have been conditioned to not interfere or disturb the frenetic affairs of men. The social structure in America offers little compensation for the individual woman, but simply reflects the neglect and abuse on a cultural scale. Even today, men may stockpile career advancements while women often support the family structure at home with domestic labor that is unrecognized and uncompensated. No matter what career path women take, the assumption of domestic duties is implicitly assigned to them. If women have a professional career, they survive in hostile competitive environments that are healthy for neither man nor woman.

In partnership, women want to trust us as men, yet the masculine impulse toward providing direction can so easily backslide into a male power-over exploitation of the feminine. Extreme cases of this dynamic can result in an opportunistic feeding frenzy of an unrealized man on the core radiance and vitality of an openly trusting woman, leaving her depleted and him temporarily bloated with his own tyranny.

Leadership or Tyranny?

Masculine core emphasis is drawn toward leadership. This masculine impulse is often seen as a hot topic because some orders of feminist thinking see it as just another example of a male dominance philosophy. The feminist skepticism is understandable because there is the undeniable issue of the general history of masculine corruption and violence. It is certain that men deserve women's scrutiny and suspicion, something men have for so long unfortunately earned. But the deeper and authentic movements of masculine and feminine expression need not be marginalized over the sake of the current masculine error.

If men are to change, they need an opportunity to make things right. To completely dismiss core masculine potency because some men have abused their station is not the answer. Though men established in their true core may be in the minority, they are also the clear power in the field. We need the full ferocity and leadership of coherent masculine men to press for change in the current field of error. We may not be able to evolve all men, perhaps not even the majority in the short term, but what we can do is set the standard for what the authentic masculine expression actually is, and reveal the lie about what it is not. We can begin to set in motion the invitation to an accessible and living male potency.

Our women are waiting for us to right the ship, to gift them a healthy masculine population to choose from. We desire and expect them to devote their lives to the bond we forge with them, yet our commitment to them has typically run nowhere near as deep. We ask all, but give much less, a paycheck perhaps, and call it even. But it is not even, and it's not right.

So we ask much of women to trust our lead, and to some women any notion of male leadership will appear as inequality and oppression. But if we ask the feminine, in absolute trust, to defer to leadership and stewardship of a coherent masculine presence that protects and serves the feminine, we may ask, where then is the tyranny? Such partnership becomes in actuality a circle of mutually influencing and empowering relational activity where neither can truly be said to be leading or following.

Masculine leadership in truth is more a tonal posturing than a dominance assertion. The masculine, like a rudder, expresses guiding action running benevolently below the surface of the relationship. The movement is definitely felt, but not always displayed. A healthy masculine will present itself as a palpable and benevolent service action that feels strong, safe, wise, decisive and dedicated to the cause. It acts proactively and without deliberation when the safety and well-being of the feminine is at risk. The healthy masculine makes considered choices and commits to them, taking a full accountability for the outcome of his actions.

I am convinced that women desire truly potent men and that they don't want, as women, to mirror masculine behavior in themselves. Many women appear frustrated and tired at trying to carry the weights and responsibilities of both sexes alone. There is a desire within these women to be released from carrying the yoke of masculine responsibility and the associated burdens that come with it. They long to melt fluidly and wildly back into the luscious feminine core that is their birthright. Yet without available coherent masculine options to suit a woman's needs, many women will continue assuming the mantle of responsibility that the unrealized men around her refuse to take accountability for.

Masculine Pundits

Commercializing masculine error into a consumer product has done little to gain the trust of women who wait for genuine results from contemporary masculine pundits. Much of what gets produced in these circles unfortunately is just more male distortion in the form of books and lectures that often preach about some sort of hyper-masculine overhaul. Provocative suggestions for men to exercise their inner "warrior," or to become "superior" by emphasizing a personal "mastery" to "overcome" limiting weaknesses often pervade the media. The misleading focus usually centers around idealizing male potency through some emphasis of personal power through a willful control of one's destiny. The narcissistic residue that pervades such personal power systems often goes unnoticed by weaker men who aspire to some sense of self-potency they feel is missing in their lives.

These so-called masculine teachers illicit intrigue with the dormant men who gather around them by pressing provocative assertions. One book suggests that men will naturally desire other women even when they are in a fully committed coupling with a female partner or that no man can put a woman before his "mission" or his work in the world. Some go so far as to tell men to ejaculate up their spine instead of through the humble urethra God provided to us to do the job.

Another popular notion is the idea that a man must shield himself from the feminine wiles of his lover, enduring her "furies" because she is inherently wired to "test" her man through calculated acts of feminine wrath. The idea is nonsense. No woman worth her perceptive salt needs to waste her energy by "testing" her man. She has ample opportunity to observe his performance amid the myriad circumstances that life will throw at him. She will observe how he handles everything, from children to traffic jams, and she will be taking precise note of every occasion until she "feels" and knows his core intimately. Never in the bonded state of the relationship following courtship does a woman consciously or unconsciously desire to "test" her man. Life will test him upfront, and if she chooses her champion wisely, the commitment to that choice then translates to a commitment to that man, which in turn concretizes his devotion to her radiance. Only fools check the temperature of the water after they jump in, and women are not fooling around when they choose to bond with a man for life.

These emphatic beliefs can breed in men an unwarranted mistrust of women, emphasizing them mainly as temptress and distraction to the masculine regime, a kind of spiritual machismo I find both distasteful and flawed. It is simply inaccurate for any man to suggest that masculine expression is weakened, diminished or in any way threatened by a healthy feminine consort. If men today are indeed lost in a jungle of distorted masculine expression, then having no guides at all would be better than having these kinds of misleading ones, because it is better to leave a lost man to his own instincts then to lead him down a path of deepening distortion.

These are critical eras we are moving through with less and less room for continued error. Our times require more from male leaders than pop perceptions that sound clever and package nicely. We have been fortunate to be gifted clear and coherent contemporary masculine guides such as Robert Bly, Sam Keen, Michael Meade and Joseph Campbell—men who scraped the belly of the male beast. These are honest men who value truth more than appearing clever. We may celebrate these teachers of men who themselves ache and yearn for a genuine understanding of the masculine condition while being leaders in the field by representing that male accounting. In their wise counsel is woven the noble trademark of men who point beyond themselves and their excellent instruction to a wisdom larger than even they may fully embody. These men bear the mark of a fierce humility that demonstrates a successful feminine integration into their core masculine.

If we are to make genuine progress toward authentic evolution of the masculine core, then we had better get serious and honest about where we actually are as men, and then make healthy choices about where we need to be. The last thing we need is to negate or dismiss the feminine while dwelling on hyper-masculine perpetuity. It is time for men to ingest the archetypal feminine we have for generations now refused to partake of. We need men who have the courage to live from the heart of a life that they accept is something fundamentally out of their absolute control. We need a band of brothers, men who have the strength to instill within themselves the potent coupling of ferocity and surrender.

Monotheism and Severing of the Feminine

No discussion of modern masculine responsibility can be legitimate without an analysis of the severe effects of the introduction and establishment of pure monotheistic religious doctrines and the profound effect they have had on men in western culture.

In monotheistic religious doctrine the masculine has been distilled by design out of the organic, whole state of the masculine/feminine polarity combination, and set aside for refinement into a compartmentalized patriarchal canon. It forms the framework of a religious platform that can serve to bolster regimes of military ambition and/or central power authority consolidation. The stark and intentional absence of the feminine in monotheistic doctrine originally served to condone, sanction and ratify martial agendas and has since set in motion a system of belief that, centuries later, appears curiously outside question or challenge.

The single-point authority affinity that monotheism has with unilateral regimes of social power in the world of men make it a natural fit for individuals who wish to rule and conquer without dissention within the rank and file of its citizenry. Singular absolute power and authority embodied by one projected male figure in heaven mesh well with totalitarian regimes ruled by singular figures of male conquest here on earth; ultimately, the pair make symbiotic sense to the strategic framework of ambitious men who seek to consolidate massive social power and affirm it with mystical sanction that cannot be argued against.

Monotheism dismisses the archetypal mystery of the fluid feminine while imposing a conceptual projection of single-point, male-embodied, anthropomorphic divinity. This masculine-appearing God rules alone with absolute authority and is purported to act directly and specifically in the world affairs of men. The God of Abraham conveniently selects a "special people," evidently assigning the rest of humanity a notably less-favored status by default.

The contemporary triumvirate that most dramatically represents monotheistic dogma today is the cousin religions of Judaism, Christianity and Islam. It is interesting to note that the major establishing figures of these religions (not necessarily the original teachers) all imposed monotheistic doctrine while facing the challenge of large military and/or power consolidation scenarios in their lifetimes.

These organizations of religious worship all invoke the gathering fold of their followers around one God, a Supreme Being who either speaks directly to selected human emissaries or sends angels or prophets to convey critical messages of ethical and moral import designed apparently to eradicate disorder and social turpitude among the masses. However, in each of these religious examples we see a uniform zero tolerance for integration of feminine qualities of the sublime, unknowable and mysterious aspects of existence that for millennia have served to balance and put into context the brittle moralistic tenets of male-born conceptual dogma.

Without integration of the critical elements of the feminine archetype into spiritual doctrine, the masculine core finds itself in a context where it cannot fully realize and activate the depths of its true potential, and the overall imbalance can make for cultural participants and leaders who may be prone to a fundamentalism and extremism that can so easily unfold toward a culture of violence.

Consider the depth and scope of such historical events as the Crusades, the Spanish inquisition, prosecutions of heresy, witch-hunting, and the conquest and eradication of native aboriginals, such as what took place in America and Australia, to name a few. All of this violence and conquest was in some way condoned and sanctioned by central-authority power paradigms that claimed to be operating in the name of a monotheistic Christian God, appropriately drawn up as a God of wrath, vengeance and righteousness. This "God" ironically seemed to serve the power regimes of the day as a justifying entity to any and all manner of human depravity that the central authority powers felt inclined to dole out.

The lack of feminine presence and influence in male-dominated, monotheistic doctrines keeps the feminine influence socially marginalized on all counts, and that alone makes the religions suspect. A culture without feminine integration knows no tonal check or balance to masculine distortion, and history bears that fact out.

The true masculine core does not marginalize the feminine, and if we are to truly evolve and unfold the authentic masculine core in men, then we will require a comprehensive feminine integration at every level of implicit and explicit expression within the human condition. It is essential that all forms of faith and worship come to embrace and include a reverential dimension of the feminine if we desire a balanced and coherent cultural expression.

Male Mojo

Being proper male stewards means not only taking care of the feminine, but also shepherding the masculine toward coherent ends. One of the major sources of masculine disintegration exists within the arena of sexuality, which is itself currently being exploited for profit by the pharmaceutical industry much in the same way that female depression is.

As young men our brains are hardwired for sex and habituated to respond to learned stimuli as well as genetically prompted impulses of attraction. Getting aroused and ejaculating are usually not problematic at this stage of sexual expression. As men age while in committed relationships, a patterned dynamic often sets in. Our repeated sexual rapport with our wives or lovers can become habitual and rote. Our ability to achieve and sustain an erection becomes diminished with the waning sense of sexual excitement we experienced before, which originally had arisen from new and fresh titillations. The sheer familiarity and informal accessibility of our monogamous partners seem to dull our sense of their living sexual draw. We find ourselves struggling to rise to the occasion of patterned lovemaking with our partner.

This is where many, many long-term couples find themselves today. And if our sexuality remains solely in the adolescent objectification/titillation realm, we will never know long-term sexual communion with our partners. Older men in particular experience the wane of hormone-based responsiveness and begin to worry that they may have lost their male mojo. What has often occurred actually has to do with the fact that sexual libido expresses itself differently at different ages.

One of the reasons young men fail to establish a coherent masculine sexuality in their youthful years is that the clarity of their core expression has become clouded by the sheer tenacity of the hormone-driven impulse they are slave to. Without skilled correction, that version of sexuality becomes distorted over the long haul, and at midlife the male body will call for a radical transformation of sexual expression to right the ship. At this point, without decades of coherent sexual practice to serve as grist for the new transformational dynamic of subtler sexual embodiment, men will simply begin to fall off sexually. The lack of cultural wisdom around this issue creates a fissure in the masculine condition that pharmaceuticals exploit, and once again a billion-dollar industry in drug manufacturing experiences another boom cycle.

Most men have little idea how lovely maturely integrated sexuality can be. It's a sad loss. The tenderness, the power, the communion, the stillness and the surrender are sources of beauty within healthy sexuality that most men never know. Being proper male stewards means rewarding our bodies as men with these nourishing baths of sexual communion.

Muting the Feminine Light

We have a responsibility to take care of our women, and yet the arsenal of antidepressants doctors and pharmaceutical companies dole out, particularly to women, has become an unfortunate norm in our culture. There is an odd projection that something is "wrong" with women for feeling despair, hopelessness, overwhelm, grief and deep sadness. But instead of addressing the root issue of the social distortions that stimulate those intense feelings, we seek instead to pathologize the emotional wounds as problematic, and create a consumer product to exploit it.

Like the lobotomy and shock treatments of the mid-20th century, we have asserted a new method to strip the life out of our girls in an effort to mute the outrage (or inrage) some women embody. When a woman demonstrates enough ferocity to step outside the box of male control paradigms and scream "no," the culture responds with dismissal and medication.

A study of antidepressant use in private health insurance plans by the New England Research Institute found that 43 percent of those who had been prescribed antidepressants had done so without any psychiatric diagnosis or any mental health care beyond the prescription of the drug. Furthermore, and perhaps even more shocking was that many of these antidepressant-prescribing physicians were not mental health physicians nor in any way formally trained or instructed to diagnose mental illness or prescribe mental health drugs.

Indeed, in 2002, according to the Center for Disease Control and Prevention, more than one in three doctors' office visits by women involved the prescription of an antidepressant, either for the writing of a new prescription or for the maintenance of an existing one. Another telling statistic was revealed in a study in the *British Journal of Psychiatry*, which reported that twice as many psychiatric drugs are prescribed for women than for men.

These statistics are alarming and point toward a trend that suggests a troubling tendency toward the drugging of our women. Today there exists an arsenal of 87 different prescription drugs for the three clinical disorders of depression, anxiety and insomnia. Are we to believe that suddenly within the last 25 years so many women have become staggeringly unable to cope with life to such a degree that they now need a huge arsenal of psychiatric drugs to cope and survive?

Pharmaceutical companies have very profitable "solutions" that end up controlling the natural life force and expression of our women. But what can we expect from a healthy adult who is being subjected to neglect or abuse? Two basic responses to oppression are submission or rebellion; the former socially acceptable and the latter an offense. By our society pathologizing rebellion, it becomes socially acceptable to drug women into submission.

The problem however isn't the response of rebellion; the problem is the original act of oppression. If we as men recognize and end the hurting, controlling and stifling of our women, we would not only heal the culture of masculine feminine relations but we would also collapse a misguided multi-billion-dollar pharmaceutical industry of psychiatric drugs overnight.

Picking Up the Pieces

Integrating a man's own internal feminine into the overall balance of his functional awareness allows a man to comprehensively understand that all things (living or inanimate) are fundamentally interconnected. When taken to heart, this perception reveals that the masculine agent must consider the whole before any actions are expressed through him. To do otherwise is to exploit, rape, abuse or neglect anything that is subject to the direct affect of his actions.

Considering the whole, before taking action in the world, is an accountability axiom of masculine embodiment that no man can be exempt from, and it is the sacred perceptive ground on which we must ultimately meet our women and the natural world that we engage. By dismissing the necessity of true intimacy with the total creative matrix, men have been able to make the violence referred to in this chapter intellectually justifiable to their half-awake conscience. Breaking life up into separate objects makes the subjects of such vile compartmentalization susceptible to a peculiar contempt—and, by extension, violence. A fully coherent and awakened masculine core could not commit such error, because the primary reality of the interconnectedness of all things is always honored, and the feel of it is never forgotten or displaced.

THE MASCULINE DESIGN
FOR SERVICE

Love is glorified most
In its deepest violation
In as much as space
Could violate the infinite.

— From *Who Is a Liar?*

Agents of Service

Matthew 6:24: "Ye cannot serve God and Mammon." The Biblical quote above is on point. If we are not serving life, then we are self-serving, and we either serve one or the other, there is no gray area. It is a good mantra to inquire moment to moment, "Who or what do I serve?" Do you commit your life to the Intelligence that created all of us, or do you bow before your own self-serving interests? Listening to the heart of life as it directs us is truly an art form; the next step is to translate that understanding into the world as action.

I remember walking out of the auditorium after "Career Day" at my high school. From one job industry booth to the next, I had just surveyed the culture's offerings for career employment. Outside, I remember shaking my head and saying, "Uh-oh, is that it?" I knew then instinctively that whatever my service was to be in the world, it certainly was not fully represented by any vocation displayed in those booths inside. I know many in the culture have felt that way at some point about the discrepancy between what they feel they have to offer in the world and what the world has to offer them as a legitimate vehicle to express it.

A fundamental premise of this book is that as men we are creatures of service and that that service is best suited for the care and protection of women, children, nature and community. Women, whose radiance we need to thrive, and the earth, whose resources we must utilize and protect to survive, ought to be the primary focus of our husbandry and stewardship. But what does male service to the feminine actually look like? What are the aspects of male service in general?

It's a fair question to ask. Men can't get pregnant. We can't give birth. We cannot physically nurse our young. Over thousands of years of evolution, men's capacity for the graceful intuitive has been marginalized in favor of a logic and reason emphasis due primarily to role designations imposed upon them by necessity. Also, men's bodies seem to be a bit larger, having in general greater muscle mass than women. Those seem to be the basics. So what does it all add up to?

For our primal male ancestors from long ago it probably meant protection and hunting. Perhaps these masculine roles led to an organic function of leadership, which by extension then cultivated logic and reason strategies to engage a fluid, and often hostile, environment. Even today leadership, protection and a strong capacity to acquire sustaining resources are seen as paternal aptitudes.

The question and capacity of masculine service in the world all seem simple and benevolent enough. What then is the problem? What then has gone awry? The answer is that men have long ago dismissed and then summarily forgotten who and what it is they are serving. No longer do men directly serve the village or the tribe as a whole. No longer do men directly serve and protect the women and children they are, by circumstance, connected to. And how can they when they are away on some job location for several days a week working for some unrelated employer? Masculine lives have become patterned exercises in abstraction.

Having lost the wisdom that once understood that we were designed for a higher service than the procuring of a paycheck, most men grope along, fragmented, lost and morbidly disconnected from themselves. As a result, these kinds of men are perpetually easy prey for the influences of the dominant social paradigm systems and institutions that make up a man's cultural environment today.

Empty men will eventually be driven to bow before and serve the interests of the disembodied social dogma, political agenda, religious indoctrination and economic despotism that all seek a position as viable authority in the social structures of the modern world we occupy. These regimes of cultural tyranny will exploit and consume all the forlorn men who have not become grounded in their own core truth.

So many potentially healthy men have in our culture been reduced to being the minions of economic totalitarianism. They look over their shoulder at the damage (to whatever degree) that their participation in empty living has caused and have only one thing to say in their defense, "I was just doing my job."

The viral nature of this position of moral deficit is painfully mirrored in the trial of Nazi war criminal Adolph Eichmann, who by his own hand had sent millions of Jews to death camps in WWII.

His infamous defense at Nuremberg was "Befehl ist Befehl," or "orders are orders." Eichmann dismissed his own accountability for the depraved atrocities he himself had committed by ascribing all responsibility to his superior's (i.e., Hitler's) mandates. Violence is almost inevitable when half-men embrace the twisted logic that evades a full accounting of their actions in the world.

Most men are not as destructive as Adolph Eichmann. However, whenever men choose to align themselves with the self-serving agendas of incoherent authority figures instead of serving leaders who themselves bow before the sublime dictates of the human heart, they become just as dangerous as their malevolent masters. Those men then become passive-aggressive elements of a peculiar sort of masculine devolution. We may not all be leaders of other men, but we must be the absolute leaders of our own conscience. Accountability and integrity are indispensable to the coherent expression of masculine duty. Orders are not simply orders, they are direction toward a specific action that we will become accountable for if and when we execute them. If any direction or order for action does not contribute to life, we as men must refuse to carry out that command at any and all cost.

The Two Phases of Coherent Masculine Service

Coherent men serve in two distinct ways, depending on their stage in life. In young adulthood, a coherent young man serves his community, tribe, culture, nation and family. His service upholds and enhances his community as well as the cultural value systems that support it. His focus is on external action for external results as he locates and reifies himself in the outward social structures he occupies.

First-stage masculine service is all about preparation for the comprehensive second-stage surrender to grace. For the man who has not yet deconstructed, outward dedication and service to wife, family, tribe and community provides decades of committed service to the feminine, preparing him for the absolute surrender that will be a required virtue during the descent into ashes, the next phase of his masculine actualization.

For a young man, building the temple of his personal identity is essential. Building his structured world, brick by conceptual brick, allows him to bring a significant offering to the altar of life at the juncture of mature male deconstruction. All that he has personally invested in with a lifetime of fervor as a young man must, by the midlife stages of his journey, be humbly let go. The army of concepts that served him well must then be disbanded and dispersed to the nether regions of his awareness field, while the residual content of the man is retained for service to God.

In the second stage, an actualized man aligns his service with the overarching Will that created him and he directs that service toward the universe he occupies. His allegiance is to the fluid Mystery and The Living Intelligence that emanates from the thread of awareness that ties him to the Creator. His external actions are predicated entirely on the coherent execution of the internal movement of listening and responding to the impersonal authority he has surrendered to and now serves.

After the resurrection of the masculine core occurring on the heels of the essential midlife deconstruction, the focus for men shifts. Now a man serves, not so much the external value systems imposed by culture, but rather a new authority unfolding from within him, a solid ground that is sourced in the ineffable Intelligence of Great Mystery.

Post-deconstruction marks an ongoing surrender that is rendered toward a fluid response to the one true ephemeral Intelligence of the Creator. A man who has come to this refined actualization of the masculine core is less goal-oriented, and more process-focused. He seeks, moreover, the coherent execution of the insights and understandings that arise as a result of his open-field access to Source Intelligence. Integrity of action means moving in tandem with that Higher Intelligence, which becomes a consistent impulse within the conscious awareness field of such men. This stage marks a whole new order of functioning in the world for men who have arrived at the fully realized masculine core.

A man's allegiance to his own coherent core means congruency with the design and action of the Creator. Through this actualization, violence is organically abated and benevolent expression finds a potent champion. A fully realized masculine core contributes to life by serving the author of it, and there is nothing more fulfilling on earth than this to any man.

The Agentive State

Men who have no established masculine core will find a disturbing vacancy when they try to locate within themselves an inner authority to draw upon. These unrealized men will no doubt find an external influence to follow and become agents of. Without a coherent masculine center established within himself, a man is floating in this hypo-agentive state in which he will be inclined to fall in line with any leader who is superficially compelling. Whether the source of that authority is coherent or not matters little to such men, and oftentimes these minions will follow the external authority figure that intimidates them most. Most men in the culture today fall into this category of abiding within the agentive state, having no core inner ground enabling them to function autonomously, and therefore they will always crave and gravitate toward some system integration where they can find their designated assignment and place in the world.

Pack and herd animals feel most comfortable when they are part of a system of social order. Within the group dynamics of animals, hierarchy is most often an essential component. The organizational development of human social structure has not currently graduated from hierarchical paradigms, but human creatures do have the capacity and potential to evolve another order of relational protocol that could refine social systems beyond power and dominance. Currently however, the bulk of our population follows the leadership of the few who are perceived to be in the legitimate positions of authority. Legitimacy of authority in human relations, however, carries a unique potential for distortion.

When human male leadership demonstrates a clear lack of benevolent authority, the legitimacy of that position ought to be challenged and the office vacated by the offending agent. Leaders who author corruption in the human arena too often escape the swift reprisal that would unfold in typical animal social systems. This is because the general cross section of human males lacks the coherent masculine core that would give substance and traction to an appropriate confrontation with corruption.

Unrealized men, to a large degree, remain obedient to flawed male leadership even when it is blatantly clear that the authority structure is corrupt and damaging to the general social fabric. The agentive state in unrealized men is so compelling that even when faced with crisis-level abominations, they will often avert their gaze from the predicaments and continue to serve the exploitive master they have chosen to defer to.

This state of agency is the fundamental obstacle to evolving the organizational dynamics of human social systems today. Our goal of evolving the human condition need not necessarily be through the abolition of hierarchical protocol in our current social systems. What is required rather is the integration of an appropriate form of social order that will instill a coherency of masculine development in the general male population that shifts masculine expression beyond a lackey-like state of agency and into a solid core of masculine self-reliance that can confront corrupt leadership.

There will always be an appropriate few who will naturally accept the mantle of organic leadership when it is required of them. Yet it is the majority of men who would make up the rank and file of the masculine community at large that we must cultivate to a self-authored accountability if we are to affect real change within the potentials of general masculine expression.

Sacred Service

A strong subjective presence is required to activate in the world, as a young man, a will-to-power that arises from an established and cultivated sense of the personal self. A robust ego is all quite essential and healthy as long as that personal self is serving a broad benevolence beyond its own self-interests. Individual action taken without consideration of others is always courting calamity. Action that is directed primarily in service to benevolent community, to heart, to truth or to God is action that is seamlessly coherent to the Universal order. When a man's choices end up degrading, directly or indirectly, the circle of living he occupies, it always garners a heavy price in the end.

The main problem with self-centered ways of being is that they are discordant, like an out-of-tune instrument in a symphony orchestra or a flat tire on a car. The entire movement of selfish expression is always vexatious and cumbersome. As such, indulging self-serving action promotes an unnecessary exposure to collateral suffering. This distress arises from the manifestations of harmonic discord due to the crosscutting of expressive acts that move against the grain of the natural order of the universal creative coherency. Put simply, to be selfish literally ruptures harmony.

It is an odd thing to consider that it appears that the Creator allows for discord, disharmony, incoherency and all manner of violence and harmful activity to express itself through humans within the overall universal design. However, to bar these darker forms of expression would perhaps invite the notion of a totalitarian God who rules out certain undesirable potentials out of a universe of open probabilities. Such a design would seem an incompatible condition for the observable design systems of a wholly quantum universe.

With such a fully open and allowing Creator, we are given the very subjective and personal option of deciding, moment to moment, the nature of our attunement and, by extension, the quality of our active expression in the world. We may not as humans have control over this life, but we do have control over our choices, and a choice for self-centered action over life-giving service is inevitably going to be painful at some point, and on some level, to the author of that choice.

Limiting consciousness to a path of selfishness as a comparative experience to an expression of full integrity always reveals the natural choice between the two. For a clear man, morality has nothing to do with how he will conduct himself in the world. Without the need for morality judgments we can legitimately decipher what action is efficient and coherent from that which is not by listening to the sublime direction of the human heart.

Serving the living presence that created us makes intuitive sense on every level. The consciousness we embody as men in this kind of sacred service moves as a fluid intelligence that brings insight, inspiration and creative brilliance to the instrument of the human mind. This resistance-free, subtle unfolding of mystical expression is our birthright as sentient creatures.

10

CORE MASCULINE POWER

Know this now, that I shall rule
And you shall play creation's fool,
To suffer so without a cure
And die even though you never were.

— From *Creation's Fool*

L'arc de Triomphe

You don't need to be rich to be a powerful man. You don't have to be a product of expensive and formal educational institutions to be an intelligent man. You don't need to have traveled the world to be a wise man. You don't have to be a general in the armed forces or a politician to be a leader among men, and as I have told numerous incarcerated men, you don't have to live in a personal prison just because you are confined inside penitentiary walls.

The fact is, there is nothing outside of you that can stop the force and potential of your birthright to occupy the world as a fully realized man, however that may look through your particular life destiny. Though there are many historically acclaimed heroes who have set the example, there are countless more men who have lived lives of relative obscurity, who have secured the inner victory as well. Joseph

Campbell referred to this arc of triumph as the "hero's journey." Hard-wired into the instinctual expression of the masculine core, and imprinted on the psychic DNA of every man, is the call to this universally male potential.

When we are boys it emerges in the form of heroic aspirations and dreams of being intrepid characters embodied by culturally derived service icons. Subsequently, soldiers, policemen and firemen become model expressions of this traditionally masculine emphasis, with the calling thematically characterized in the common police slogan, "to protect and to serve."

Three qualities need to be present in the male aspirant to manifest the requisite heroic proportion. The first is heart, which translates to an uncompromising value of care and honor for all that is sacred. The second is ferocity, that particularly male activation that drives an unflinching commitment and tenacious application to a particular cause. And the third is integrity, the purity of action that does not get compromised or diluted by worldly distractions. For the Knights of the Round Table, only Galahad commands all of the requisite qualities, and therefore in due course he alone acquires the Holy Grail.

Adherence to these three ideals—heart, ferocity and integrity—will help catapult boys fully into the arena of young men. However, these virtues only bring on the game. Full-scale mature masculine integration takes the better part of a lifetime spent deepening the application of the coherent masculine.

A lifetime that demonstrates a sincere expression of purity in character and fierce devotion to the self-actualized mission separates the "Galahad Men" from the merely well-intentioned. The Holy Grail abhors tentative souls, and the authentic hero must ultimately have no residue of personal reservation about his absolute commitment to the heart of life itself. Indeed, his conversion to full masculine embodiment is dependent on it.

The fires of spirit will, in due course, burn all impurity out of the willing man, and only the utter surrender of the Christ-like heart-warriors will complete the full arch of triumph in this life. Every man instinctively reconciles the sublime fiat of this heroic passage in his own way. Whether he engages the journey or not, and how deeply he moves toward the transforming power of it, is his business with life.

Hyper-masculine and Hypo-masculine

Common notions view the masculine and feminine polarities as though they were "either/or" expressions. But it is an error to assume that as a human we embody either one or the other, because both genders are each designed to contain healthy measures of the masculine and feminine.

Men who emphasize the masculine core must also own and integrate the often less-emphasized portion of the feminine within them. Indeed, any man who has realized his true masculine core will have already reconciled that portion of the feminine within himself. This feminine integration is not just a nice complement to masculine expression, it is a necessary function of it.

Of course it stands to reason that if there is a majority of men who lack feminine integration, there is a minority of men who may inversely lack the requisite masculine integration. These kinds of men often possess a deficiency in initiative, drive, passion and ferocity—a kind of hypo-masculine condition. But for the men lacking healthy masculine integration, the movement toward reconciling it is different than for those who need to integrate the feminine. The process for men actualizing a lost masculine becomes a bit like finding the sunglasses you misplaced or the old basketball you stored away in the attic so long ago—the action is described more as one of reclamation than integration. Men need only to remember the natural masculine affinity that they were born with. The feminine within them however, requires cultivation.

The man who has succeeded in opening to his masculine polarity, but without the requisite feminine archetypal virtues first having been wholly assimilated by him, will struggle with this imbalance. Embodying fully potent manhood always requires reconciling the feminine within. This is the miss most men make on the masculine journey.

A personal trainer friend of mine down at my gym pulled me aside one day. He noticed something about my regimen. Over the years of my lifting in the gym it appears that there had been a failure on my part to develop and activate the full complement of muscle systems in my entire shoulder region. On the surface they looked healthy, but, in fact, inside there had been a significant imbalance that was leading to a resulting chronic pain, which I confessed to him. He explained it all to me.

The shoulder, it turns out, is a very complex system. There are smaller muscle groups deep within the shoulder that I wasn't aware of. These minor muscle groups needed target specific activity beyond the four basic power lifts I had been employing to maintain the region. Failure to engage these smaller muscle groups while simultaneously increasing the mass and strength of the major muscles of the shoulder that surround them results in a structural dilemma that manifests itself as pain because the entire complex of shoulder muscles moves as a whole.

This oversight of mine was a typically classic male blunder, and it mirrors closely the error in our overall functioning as men. Overdeveloping the obvious masculine facets of expression to a hyper-masculine state while simultaneously neglecting the subtler complementary feminine aspects of coherent male embodiment is the main reason that core male power fails to fully actualize to potential in men.

As men we can achieve a rudimentary functioning day to day, even if out of balance, and many of us are content to do just that. But, as with my shoulder, a potential for pain-free power and a full potential of expressed excellence can never be achieved without holistic integration and refinement of both of the polarities within us. So I am suggesting to the men who read this book what I have suggested to very large and formidable men in prison: investigate, look deeper, engage and reconcile the dormant feminine within to deepen the understanding and efficacy of the core masculine.

My '67 Chevelle or Your Life

Of my work in prison with inmates, one story always stands out in my mind. I was facilitating a group discussion about what power for a man really means. One inmate spoke up and said, "It's like why I'm up in here. I kill't a man 'cuz he was sitt'n on the hood of my '67 Chevelle. Now I asked him once to get off, and that car was fuckin' cherry. That motherfucker just dissed me, and I kill't his ass, and I'd do it again."

"So that's your example of power?" I asked.

"Yeah, I showed that fuck who's got the power," he replied.

I went on to ask him if he was married at the time or if he had a girlfriend. He said he was married at the time and had had two kids with his wife.

Then I said this to him, "So one guy sits on your car, blows you off when you tell him to move and so you kill him, and now you're down for life inside this shit hole. Can't make love to your wife. Can't raise your children. Can't live your life a free man all because one chump dissed you? You call that power? Sure, he's dead all right, but you're living the rest of your life in a prison. And why? Because you were unable to make a clear choice in that moment, and you reacted instead from a hot head. In that instant, your inability to make a clear grounded choice caused your family to have their father and husband taken away from them."

I acknowledged that he had obviously demonstrated physical power over his victim as represented in his lethal act, but I suggested also that he had had no real power over the moment to choose wisely, to choose something that ran deeper.

I then said, "I've got no gripe with your capacity to apply lethal force where and when it's needed. I actually respect that ability when there is a real call for that degree of action. My suggestion to you is that there is a difference between the reactive application of raw force and a fully realized masculine power that can discern whether or not to use it. And that's what I'm talking about when I say 'power.' It's the capacity a man has to move coming from a place of broader understanding and consideration, instead of just reacting off a bundle of heated emotion."

I finished by honoring his value around respect. "That guy who sat on your car, I don't like his behavior any more than you do, believe me, but you and your family weren't worth the cost of setting him straight for good—not in my eyes anyway."

Speaking that bluntly in a prison may not seem like the safest thing to do, but this man didn't throw down on me like he did the fool who sat on his Chevelle. In fact, the words sank quickly into his heart, and I could see a sobriety move across his face as the understanding took hold. I felt a deep compassion for his blind spot the moment he recognized it as such. True masculine power is not what most men think it is, but once they are shown the distortion relative to the truth, they often recognize it immediately. For most men this discovery is a bitter pill to have to swallow, but a necessary one if we are to evolve as men.

Ferocity Versus Violence

Healthy masculine is fierce by nature. When I say fierce, I am speaking about a quality that allows men to apply themselves to the occasion of their own lives with a singular devotion, a raw passion that manifests itself as a powerfully undeniable authority in action. In this way, men become aligned with their own hearts, and as they become fixed in their core as men, they express their lives with a directed benevolent intensity.

But that kind of ferocity can only come on the heels of a consecrated service to life. Men cannot actualize such a commitment until they burn away the lies and confusion that can end up surrounding and fragmenting their lives. Men need to seek out the truth of their own core expression amid the morass of cultural error and assert it.

Unfortunately, too many men have chosen to give in to flawed cultural values instead of surrendering through the feminine into the heart of life. Without feminine integration, the virile coherent ferocity of men will become dumbed down, and ultimately express itself as lopsided male fits of aggression, control and domination. This violence is perpetuated by the existing male hegemony that persists in the culture.

It may sound counterintuitive, but men need access to the authentically fierce dimension of their being before they can successfully be compassionate, tender, loving and wise, because this kind of ferocity is not really about aggression. True masculine ferocity is actually the organic determination and commitment to action that arises out of a grounded authority that is sourcing from the heart of life.

The fiercest men I have ever known were internally fluid and still creatures. When a call to action was upon them, a torrent of indomitable power emerged effortlessly. Men in general have yet to fully tap into the core of true male ferocity in our current evolution. It is exciting and hopeful to consider that the deepest potency of embodied masculine expression could be yet to come.

Establishment versus Conquest

In the words of Isaac Asimov, change is the only constant. With regard to human beings, the inevitability of socio-cultural advancement over time seems natural and appropriate. But it turns out that through the centuries, the development of the human condition has most dramatically displayed itself as historic cycles of human conquest that have revealed themselves to be little more than sophomoric exercises in empire consolidation. Aggressive campaigns of external power acquisition have little to do with movements that evolve human consciousness toward its ultimate victory. We as a species have experienced a continual unfolding spasm of control-seeking conquest and decline throughout history, with perhaps a minimal current of the human affairs within flowing toward the ends of an enriched human condition.

To evolve with a conscious intention toward the finest in human potential requires an establishment of a new order of functioning that emerges as obvious and necessary from the limiting paradigms of the past. There is no way for men to find through conquest an evolutionary refinement that would arise naturally as a result of coherent functioning in the world. Establishing the living beauty in human expressive potential is far more dynamic than conquering the static paradigms of men. There is more victory in realizing our human potential than any achievement that the martial affairs of men could ever garner, because there is no beauty in raw conquest and no abiding truth in worldly power. Indeed, establishing beauty is the forgotten legacy of the masculine archetype. Conquering civilizations and people has been, and is, the indulgence of distorted and broken men.

For contemporary men, the very notion of victory itself must evolve. Our victory must first be over our own limitations as men, not the conquest of others for worldly gain. For each man today, fear itself has become the great destroyer, fulfilling its own fretful prophesies and driving individuals to dark and desperate activities. For the new champions of coherent masculine expression, it will not be enough to merely confront our fears before we act. Those who will know true victory in life must commit totally to the act itself despite all possibility of fearful outcomes. Within such action lies the establishment of an authentic human triumph that prevails no matter what the results.

Authority:
Pre- and Post-deconstruction

Male ferocity as expressed through the coherent subjective persona of a healthy younger male will find its allegiance rooted to the community. A coherent young man's actions and values will be derived from, and guided by, the traditional heritage of his source culture.

Young men, because they have not yet met midlife deconstruction, will express action through the lens of the subjective world they have come to know. Their authority will come from a connection to the cultural heritage and traditions they serve. The momentum of a benevolent cultural tradition and the affirmation of its ancestral legacy provide the necessary authority a young man needs to activate with potency in the world.

The fully deconstructed elder man, however, knows a different order of authority in his life. Male ferocity as expressed through such fully realized men is rooted in the fluid dictates of the ineffable human heart and owes its allegiance to the mystical Creative Intelligence that has sourced all things. Post-deconstructed men find their authority sourced entirely in the will of the Creator, which they now feel moving inside them, moment to moment. This measure of masculine actualization is in a class all its own, and too few men today achieve its embodiment.

If a post-deconstructed man finds himself in a coherent culture, his heart's alignment with the ineffable Intelligence will fold harmoniously into the culture's call for contributing action, and his duty to "God and Country" will reconcile.

If however, the realized man finds himself a product of a corrupt culture, an incompatibility arises by virtue of his clarity in thought and deed, confronting the errors of the distorted social paradigms that surround him. Realized men who find themselves in this context are often either exalted or condemned, or both, by the prevailing social power structures.

The Example of Jesus

Historically, Christ is seen as an individual who arose in a religious state and was often identified as a rabbi, a spiritually anointed one who gave testimony to a new order of religious doctrine.

Yet Christ lives deeper than religion, he perceives the truth of his own heart. He embraces what he understands to be the will of God as expressed through his own particular life force. The vision he sees regarding his core redemptive mission will sweep through millennia of centuries, touching billions of human hearts in a way no mere human religious figure could ever have. This leading of humanity out of its darkness deeply engages Christ's masculine core in a way no mere religion ever could. In the realization of this moment, the total expression of Jesus Christ is actualized; he is not to be confined to the parameters of his culture, he is a pure son of The Light, and his destiny is clear.

Christ's example shines as a complete model of true actualization of the masculine core in its first and second stages. The vision and execution of his mission move congruent with the will of the Intelligence that creates him. His absolute dismissal of personal enhancement through worldly gain reveals a masculine core fully surrendered to the feminine, and desiring only to serve the natural order of creation by bowing to the impersonal will of the Creator itself. The demonstrative and radical deconstruction of Christ's subjective residues begins in the desert, achieves its apogee at Gethsemane and completes itself in the powerful metaphoric symbology of the Crucifixion.

Being rooted in his true life's work and manifesting a purity of fidelity to his calling unrivaled by any man, Christ actualizes his ordained legacy, which becomes a force unparalleled in human history, blasting through century after century so that the living potency of his intensely authentic life is felt intimately and passionately to this day.

It is ironic that, amid the living promise of Christ's fierce example, so many Christian men's lives could continue to move palely and shallowly through an abyss of passive mediocrity. But then again, Christians rarely talk about Christ in terms of his being ferocious about anything. History, however, clearly affirms that in Jesus the intensity of his masculine core was energized to a radically free state through the influence of a complete feminine integration. We witness the feminine mystique alive in Jesus when he moves mystically outside of religious doctrine and political zeitgeist, or when he responds fluidly and intuitively to the storied occasions of his life. The feminine balance prompts him to be stirred deeply by a compassion for suffering that recognizes the inherent unity of all things, great and small. And most profoundly, the feminine asks everything of him as he sublimates his personal will to the unfolding design of the Creator, even unto death.

And yet we see the masculine at work in him as well. Jesus chooses of his own volition to return provocatively to Jerusalem where he had enemies in high places. He enters defiantly through the east wall portico of the city mounted on a donkey, taunting the sacred Jewish prophesies of Zechariah regarding the coming Messiah. He flips over the tables of the moneychangers in the temple. Christ communes with repentant harlots and tax collectors. He refuses to flee to safety the night before his imminent Roman arrest and seizure. He refuses to give Pontius Pilate the easily rendered, politically appropriate answers that would garner his release from condemnation. These actions are neither passive nor particularly peace-oriented; these are the defiant, inflammatory, provocative gestures of an incredibly ferocious and masculine-emphasized persona.

The passive, humble, somber, martyr-like Jesus persona that pervades much Christian dogma is an unfortunate rendering of a very radical and passionate spirit. Pilate did not condemn a victim of circumstance to the cross on Golgotha, Jesus confirmed and participated in his destiny. Those in the seats of power in Jerusalem were trying to destroy a social influence that the Pharisees could not predict or control, and Jesus was hardly playing it safe.

The sheer force of expression embodied by the vessel of pure integrity we call Jesus Christ ought to take its place in history as an inspiration of masculine authority attuned to its highest calling. We as men in particular would do well to take notice of, and be inspired by, the incredibly virile and potent masculine example that Jesus truly represents, for along with Jesus' tenderness and depth of compassion come also his fierce integrity and boldness of action directly in the face of life-threatening consequences.

The sheer magnitude and scope of Christ's affect on the human condition 2,000 years after his death are a testimony to the raw potential of fully realized masculine expression when appropriately integrated with the feminine. The balance that results from Christ's inner reconciling enhances his dimensionality and potency exponentially in the world, and his brief but powerful ministry proclaimed that possibility as available to everyone.

Relevance

When a man's actions lose efficacy, he becomes irrelevant, and his social gravitas becomes defunct. Irrelevance can occur organically through the physical incapacitation of extreme old age, or through a man's own failure to realize his true masculine core within his given productive lifetime.

Also, for any individual, relevance can come and go with time when that relevance is not embodied consciously. Unconscious relevance occurs when charismatic and dynamically talented men gain insight and creative brilliance through grace but fail to embody the inspired intelligence that moves through them.

Flash-in-the-pan artists, old-guard political leadership and once-extraordinary minds who have become stagnant and inert around their own prior genius are examples of individuals who lose relevance in the eyes of society because they no longer author the fresh and original content that arises from the fluid fountainhead of the One Living Intelligence.

Brilliance and creative achievement often precede morbid inertia in unrealized men because often such men feel as if they have "arrived" when accolades and notoriety follow strokes of acclaimed expression. But if they imagine that they have arrived somewhere, then they no longer are going anywhere, and the fluid stream of human evolution and creative potential will no longer utilize such individuals as coherent instruments of inspired expression.

No creative output can reflect genius in it when it has lost its inspiring current. The muses are fickle and will not be possessed or controlled. So it is that men who are not in their true masculine core cannot long be custodial stewards of creative brilliance. Creative brilliance, insight and inspiration can strike anyone at any time, but it takes a man dialed into a coherent masculine core to run these forces consistently and consciously through his instrument without the residue of the personal self contaminating, degrading or destroying it.

When men try to identify with and lay claim to the beautiful actions that move through them by grace, they disconnect from the current of luminous insight that was the very genesis of their inspired expression in the first place.

Men move soullessly in these instances where they attempt to control the creative properties of the mystical. They begin to draw straight lines to illustrate the flow of water. They employ strategies of formula to try and desperately replicate production of prior success, hoping to mimic the effects of true inspiration. By degree, they become the veritable "has-beens" of the culture, reduced to a groping performance that demonstrates mostly a pathetic effort to try and replicate what once came naturally and fluidly by grace.

It is sad to witness these washed-up men who once embodied a fresh and living expression, for they become, in time, reduced to stale composites of prior acclaim that no longer inspire or encourage the human condition. In due course they become laden with themselves, no longer useful instruments of life, no longer relevant to the culture and society.

And yet the error is unnecessary. We can as men remain vital, relevant and prolific. What is required of all men is the coherent surrender to the Creative Intelligence that inspires us. What is required is a sacrifice of the personal structure at the altar of the feminine.

11

SUBLIMATION THROUGH THE FEMININE

Shackles on a painted man
Blood that drips like dew
And for this test, there is no rest
Not for the chosen few.

— From *The Chosen*

Full Stop

An accurate examination of the masculine crisis today reveals no particular deficiency in purely male sensibilities; the predicament ironically stems from a lack of feminine balance and integration within each individual man. To focus more and more on the emphasis of hyper-masculine traits as a remedy to the current masculine crisis is a bit like adding salt to bacon. The current missing link of coherent masculine expression in the culture is actually the feminine component.

Our social structures today usually do not inculcate young men from the very beginning to integrate the feminine into their core masculine expression, and so they develop the typical hyper-masculine dynamics that distort the general cross section of young males today. Without a consistently ongoing and fluid integration of the feminine balance influencing male actualization, men at stages need to be stopped and redirected toward a prompted equalization of a more balanced polarity expression. Unfortunately, the average unbalanced man will not naturally self-restrain or self-desist to induce a complement of healthy polarity correction. As a result, contemporary hyper-masculine men need to have the momentum of their typical outward orientation of masculine expression given pause, and that is exactly what the feminine, through ritualized events, can do.

Tribal cultures catalyzed feminine equalization measures in men through periodic life-stage rituals, all involving some poignant encounter with different aspects of the feminine. Generally speaking, the feminine has the inherent capacity to stop a man in three very useful and archetypal ways. The first is with death, the second with beauty and the third with mystical awe.

Feminine as Destroyer: the Adolescent Passage

Adolescent rites of passage to manhood always require some element of blunt confrontation with mortality. Mortality in this instance becomes the aspect of the feminine that displays the terrible destructive potential of the feminine embodied best in the Hindu goddess Kali, who is the birther and destroyer of all things. Leading up to this passage, an adolescent boy has integrated only the nurturing expression of the Kali form, as embodied by his own mother. Now he will meet Kali's terrible aspect as destroyer, bringing a necessary balance of the complete feminine as an integration to his budding masculine core.

For the young male initiate, his newly formed subjective paradigm is his entire world. Facing the loss of his life means risking everything he has come to know and the would-be loss of so much he has yet to experience. Death becomes the ultimate adversarial figure to test a young man's character. This is why for young men, the feminine as destroyer is the ultimate stopping instrument. All his bluster and young bravado will be cut clean through by the stark realization that it all could be over in an instant. Without a reserve of fulfilling memories to draw upon from a richly lived life, young men are, at a gut level, appalled at the idea of risking their lives, and the sense of urgency around living in the immediate face of death becomes intense. It is this intensity engaged for reasons of service to community that will forge in the young man the alchemized elements that will propel him through the passage from boyhood to manhood.

Bringing an adolescent on the threshold of manhood to a full internal stop is no easy task. The leverage required for such an undertaking arises from exposure to the feminine as destroyer, because only she possesses the requisite influence that can give such youthful dynamism a healthy pause. "Stopping" a young man at this stage means causing him to access a still-point within himself that makes a profound life choice without the squalor of youthful drama influencing it. That clear choice of an act of service to community, made against all obvious instincts for self-preservation, will place the critical keystone of masculine activation into the foundation of a young man's life.

Feminine as Beauty:
the Marriage Passage

It is the classic depiction: a young man in the middle of his daily tasks sees a young woman and, for some reason, his whole world stops.

Men need to be stopped by beauty for several vital reasons. A man needs to be reminded of the inherent beauty beneath the substratum of his toiling existence, something that gives his labor in life dimension and purpose. He needs also to feel the exquisite beauty that nature brings forth so that it may serve to temper his fierce capacities with tenderness. But most of all he needs to feel himself empty of himself, drained out of all the worldly affairs that so consume his moment-to-moment existence, and in this way he can, if only for a few moments, become completely empty and open to beauty without restraint or guard.

If a woman strikes a young man this way he will find her marriage-worthy, and if the romantic courtship that follows reveals the requisite compatibility, there is a strong chance that in due course he will propose. He is in effect bonding to the source of the feminine radiance that has been capable of stopping his entire world with a glance, and that medicine is essential for a coherent masculine life because, as I have said in earlier chapters, men are loathe to self-desist.

And yet it is essential that they do learn to stop. It is critical for men that they become intimately fluid with the capacity for stillness within themselves. For younger men, who are busy building their lives, the feminine as beauty contains the requisite archetypal power to stop the fevered ambitions of young men in their tracks. The periodic cessation of the ambitions of the masculine psyche is necessary and critical, for if a young man continues on indefinitely in hypermasculine mode without wedding his emotional and physical body to the feminine, he will in due course become hardened, disconnected and volatile.

After marriage, many men are again stopped by beauty when their children are born. New fathers especially are softened and opened at the wonder and beauty of the new life they are so intimately connected to. Inspiring stillness in men is an important function of the feminine as beauty. Consider the dazzling array of brilliant colored petals that adorn the typical flower, which serves to attract worker bees for pollination. Without such beauty to captivate and draw our full attention, much masculine expression would be lost to rudderless activity that knows no allegiance to a life of benevolent service.

Feminine as Mystical: the Midlife Deconstruction

In midlife a man is stopped by the wall of the middle-aged transition crisis. Now the feminine will reveal itself to men as the rapturous mystical awe at the stage in their lives when they are ready for the descent into ashes. To stop the masculine momentum here, the feminine appears not as birther/destroyer as it did in the adolescent passage, not as beauty in manifestation as it revealed itself in the marriage passage, but now as the ineffable void—the great silent emptiness. This time the feminine presents itself as the great mystery beyond all human comprehension and apprehension. To fulfill this communion a man will surrender his entire being at the altar of the Absolute, and the nature of his surrender comes in the form of the total deconstruction of the subjective personal self.

In the *Bahgavad Gita* (a part of the great Hindu Sanskrit epic, the *Mahabharata*), before conducting battle, Arjuna begs Lord Krishna to let him behold his complete and total Divine nature. He wishes in effect to gaze directly upon the Godhead with mortal eyes. Arjuna can in no way, from the limited perception of his subjective personal paradigm, fathom the full import and consequence of his request.

Lord Krishna counsels him away from the appeal, but the insistent Arjuna will not be denied. Krishna as the Supreme Being complies and the theophany, or manifestation of a deity, reveals itself to Arjuna's conceptual mind as the omnipresent totality of the Supreme Being in its magnificent Universal form, with all the material of existence and the radiance of a thousand suns therewith.

Arjuna, having beheld the full spectacle of the Divine in form, is now compelled to abandon all forms of previously assigned Dharma (i.e., worldly duty) and in due course surrenders fully to the Supreme Being.

This story is a symbolic representation of the midlife deconstruction of the subjective paradigm, with an awe-inspiring mystical union serving as the catalyst toward total surrender. Confrontation with the mystical feminine is the essential element for the absolute razing and restructuring of male midlife momentum.

At this stage of a man's life he is most likely in his middle years, having arrived at the juncture where there is nothing left in the external world that compels his sense of meaning enough to fulfill the drawing sense of profound discontent within. He is ready for the internal communion of rapture with the mystical feminine that will deliver him across the threshold of his limited personal paradigm and into the broader field that will unfold the final potent chapters of his destined masculine expression.

ARCHETYPES AND GENDER ROLES

We are deeper than the Gods
Because we have chosen to wrap ourselves in flesh
And fall asleep in separateness.
We suffer the night,
Drunk with the ways in which love completes itself.

— From *Love Completes Itself*

Equality and Personhood

Discussions of sexual equality and "personhood" often end up watering down the dynamic contrast between the masculine and feminine polarities, a contrast that is absolutely essential for our attraction, bonding and current evolution. It is not wise to try and dismiss the natural contrast of masculine and feminine polarities by espousing uniform equality between the sexes on all counts. I am writing this book on men and the masculine core precisely because men and women are not the same, except in our shared humanness.

In fact, equality between the masculine and feminine will never mean that they are the same. What equality does mean is that men and women are both worthy of the same dignity, respect and opportunity to live full lives that allow them to express their complete potential as human beings.

On the other hand, women and men are hardly from different planets. We are not so foreign to one another that we cannot possibly relate to the opposite sex without first reading an instruction manual on the opposing gender. Relating to the opposite sex does not require that we become the same, nor does it mean that we must dramatically press ourselves into trying to figure out some supposed alien nature engendered by the opposite sex.

Men and women are naturally inclined to understand one another. We all embody a balance of masculine and feminine archetypal expression within our bodies, regardless of gender. Symbiotic rapport is spontaneous and inevitable when expressed between two coherent individuals of opposing polarity. The battle of the sexes is mostly a contrived entertainment vehicle; it is a manufactured war of conceptual paradigms waged among distorted representations of both polarities. Playing women against men has nothing to do with any accurate representations of the sexual archetypes. Lampooning the subject does however make for good drama and, as such, gender relations have become an object of significant consumer exploitation, even in the self-help marketplace.

Polarity Emphasis

Convention means little more than what is customary and, with regard to gender roles, it is valuable to understand that nothing is absolute. It also means that that there is no right or wrong way to inhabit a human body. In determining typical ways of expressing gender, it is important to appreciate diversity and not fall into a trap of rigid thinking about the way things are "supposed" to be.

In both homosexual and heterosexual relationships, gender polarities are at play because the masculine and feminine archetypes exist together in both men and women. The key, however, lies in which archetype a particular individual will choose to dominantly express.

As one example, a woman may embrace her masculine core as her dominant expression. If she is heterosexual, she will by nature be drawn to a straight man who has chosen to emphasize his feminine core as dominant. If she is lesbian and emphasizing her masculine core, she will by nature be drawn to a woman who emphasizes her feminine core.

Regardless of sexual orientation the attraction is almost always toward the opposite polarity dynamic, as when a masculine core emphasis pairs with a feminine core emphasis, no matter the gender designation or sexual orientation.

The old axiom that opposites attract was never truer than with the masculine and feminine cores. When it comes to coupling, bodies and sexual preferences themselves seem to matter much less in their designated assignments than does the actual emphasis of either the masculine or feminine core expression in the individual involved.

In the larger perspective, it is helpful to separate out the actual profile of masculine expression from the sense that it must be associated with a male body. The same goes for feminine expression. A core feminine emphasis need not be associated with a female body. The pure traits of masculine and feminine archetypal expression are available to either women or men—as is the choice to emphasize one or the other regardless of gender. We would all do well to recognize that neither gender has any legitimate proprietary claims on polarity emphasis.

As a matter of simplicity, *Razing Men* refers a lot to men who have chosen to emphasize the masculine core, but certainly not all men need to emphasize a masculine core to be realized men. Indeed, men do not need to be heterosexual to be coherent men. What this book explores directly is what it means to embody a masculine core emphasis, and it speaks consistently about men who embody that core emphasis as a matter of example. It bears repeating that no one way of being in the world is any more natural than another.

Androgens are people who defy gender role compartmentalization by emphasizing qualities of both masculine and feminine within a singular individual. With gender and sexuality, nothing is etched in stone. In my travels I once met a man in Great Britain who was decidedly asexual. He was physically male, no doubt. He dressed like a man and was not what I would describe as demonstrably effeminate. But, as he explained to me in conversation, he had no core sexual emphasis, one way or the other. He was in fact very pleasant to be around, and it seemed to me almost as if the lack of sexual tension in his life was unspokenly liberating. I noted a lovely even and balanced quality about him. Afterwards, I found myself asking myself some interesting questions regarding my impressions of him. Did he represent an anomaly? Did he suffer some deficiency? Or perhaps was he a glimpse of the embodiment of a form of advanced evolution of core polarity expression in human beings?

Beyond Polarities:
a Peek into the Future

I might suggest that, through the course of human evolution, core polarity expressions will eventually reach the zenith of their complimentary opposition to one another. Pair bonds then will produce exquisitely clear and fully contrasted couplings, demonstrating dramatically the splendid potential of compatibility exchange between the masculine and feminine polarities.

Beyond that point, further evolution may see the polarities that exist within each individual begin to slowly come into balance, with less and less emphasis between the genders at one or the other polarity. An age of androgyny could begin to unfold, where the tendency toward masculine or feminine emphasis in a single individual will recede. At this phase of evolution, human beings would settle into a more balanced androgynous expression of both polarities within themselves. Sexuality could evolve as well to accommodate the shift. Humans might begin to explore the relatively subtle androgynous exchanges of sexual communion, replacing the dramatically opposing dynamic that occurred during the preceding era of polarity contrast.

One can feel the textures of this vision in the book, *Left Hand of Darkness*, by Ursula Le Guin, who explores a race of androgens set on the planet, Winter. In it she beautifully elucidates the sublime rapture of androgyny, "Light is the left hand of darkness, and darkness is the right hand of light. Two are one, life and death, lying together like lovers." The exquisite completion of androgyny is a lovely vision to consider because a human being who retains a balance of masculine and feminine sexuality within his or herself leans less on another human being for a sense of completeness. That way of relating directs more weight on an individual's own existential roots, driving him or her deeper into a balanced expression. Ultimately, a more even distribution within any relational load creates a more stabilized reaching capacity to extend higher up to the heavens while laterally communing in the physical.

The Evolving
Masculine Archetype

Much of what has been written concerning men and men's work has been drawn from scholars reviewing archetypal mythologies that arose out of a budding human culture occurring over the last 5,000 to 10,000 years.

C.J. Jung, who coined the term "archetype," meant it as a momentum of common human expression that ran consistently, regardless of time, space or culture—a fundamental thread of human relatedness that ran underneath conscious expression and transcended ethnic diversity.

But why do we assume that archetypes are static? So many scholars, in discussing modern male activation, merely point to ancient mythologies and assume that those archetypal expressions are still alive and well today in exactly the same form. I'm not so sure they all are. "Warrior," "hunter," "priest" and "king"—these are some typical masculine myth archetypes that get imposed upon contemporary men. As with every other phenomenal expression, I assume archetypes are likewise evolving and have been since the dawn of humankind. An aspect of redeeming the masculine core then means distilling an extraction from only those older archetypal forms that still remain relevant today, as well as recognizing what archetypal phenomena have evolved to something new in the current phase of the contemporary masculine.

We must also understand that, in a quickly changing world in which different men are demonstrating more complex evolutions of archetypal expression, it is getting harder and harder to find the "magic bullets" from the pantheon of masculine archetypes and attempt to utilize them solely as the universal key to all male unfolding. It is perhaps more to the point to see archetypes as stylistic expressions of the human condition that may be fundamental, but not necessarily always essential to core masculine expression. For in the final analysis, focusing on any particular archetypal expression may reveal more of an abstraction than any concrete utensil we can utilize in apprehending the epitome of core masculine expression.

The truth is that all archetypes function best as a default response tool for the unconscious actor, because archetypes simply flavor the human awareness field but are not the substantive content of it. The man in his true masculine core is a man who is impeccably awake and is not ruled by the unconscious dynamics where all archetypes reside. However an understanding of these qualifying impulses as men will ultimately allow us to better utilize our heritage of human instinct toward a more coherent end.

13

SEXUALITY

For all that we are
Would laugh at near and far
And separation
Between the stars.

— From *When I Say Goodbye*

Physiology and Energy

The Buddha is purported to have admitted that if there were two worldly desires as potent as lust to reconcile, he might not have attained liberation at all. Sex may be one of the most instinctively hard-wired mechanisms in the human condition. As an embodiment of masculine emphasis, sex is a huge responsibility because we masculine agents often initiate sexual activity as we move into the receptivity of the feminine.

Unfortunately, masculine-emphasized expression has been missing a key integration. That is because we are typically not informed much at all about sex in general as young men, and certainly we are never informed that sex is fundamentally an energetic act. The common, primary focus on sensory arousal, erotica titillation and the tactile application of genital stimulation is merely the neurological version of sex. This kind of single-dimension intercourse will

173

inevitably erode both partners' vitality. A woman will find her radiance depleted slowly by degree if she continues to indulge in this kind of hyper-masculine sex.

As is the case with most expressive forms of the human condition today, contemporary sexual paradigms are sorely lacking the incorporation of the feminine polarity. Masculine-emphasized men have not yet consciously discovered what arousal feels like within themselves, especially when that arousal moves apart from physical stimulation, sensory titillation, fantasy and erotica.

Until these kinds of men experience what it means to have their sexual arousal arise from the implicitly intimate and living connection a man consciously feels with his beloved, he cannot know or co-create the full potential of lovemaking. To know this experience, he must embrace the feminine within himself and integrate its fluid nature into his full expression as a man. Masculine qualities that express themselves in sexuality as agendas of control, goal orientation, and methodical and mechanistic form must give way to the balancing influence of surrender, moment-to-moment presence and a fluid response.

Sexual consummation within this more balanced context feels very different for a mature man than it does for a young man. In a more refined sexual rapport, there is less climax orientation pushing the body toward an agenda of male orgasm. Rather, there is more a kind of connective current that loops between the lovers, forming a sexual dynamic that is driven by the deep polarity exchange moving between the two.

Receptivity and Response

Receptivity to the coherent masculine by the feminine is a natural dynamic of sexuality. This receptivity is also probably the most obvious point at which exploitation of the feminine occurs by the unskillful masculine in the dance of sexuality.

Initiating action is the realm of the masculine archetype. However, with unintegrated men and women, the natural receptivity of the feminine is often confused with an act of submission, and what could be a healthy communal act often digresses into some kind of eroticized power exchange. As a result, in such contexts of unbalanced intercourse, men and women often miss the more fulfilling natural and organic sexual dynamic.

In coherent heterosexual communion, a man's energy runs through a woman during the act of consummation. She allows herself to completely let go into the irrational and groundless swirl of the raw feminine she emphasizes. She seeks to become seeded (if even metaphorically) with the power and fire of the male energy she is receiving.

For a man, the sheer vivacity of her unrestrained core receptivity leaves a mark on his soul, an experience that moves far deeper than mere enchantment. The depth of her reception to his masculine core is affecting his overall masculine activation. He will feel enhanced by her acceptance and celebration of his particular masculine essence. The fierce masculine in him may desire her radiance as a lover and feel moved to protect it from corruption.

The protection and desire aspect of the male becomes a key component to the continued sexual draw of the feminine toward her masculine partner. If it fails to manifest, or wanes with time, a feminine-emphasized partner feels neither safe nor completely attracted. Her whole body will not crave him if he does not display a capacity for this particular quality of masculine ferocity.

Fierceness here is not related to male aggression, but rather the ability to engage in potent and healthy male action when it is needed. A man's capacity to act with efficacy in the world causes the feminine to relax and open in his presence. A feminine-emphasized woman intuitively requires fire with which to bond, and coherent potent male action demonstrates and represents the "fire" she seeks.

As a divorce mediator I have seen on occasion when a woman's soon-to-be ex-husband enters the room, and the mere physical proximity of him immediately begins to drain the life and radiance out of her. It is a sad thing to witness—to see a man to whom she once promised her life now having this depleting affect on her.

For our part as men, fully sexually connecting to a woman requires an openness to her that feels and relates to her entirety. Acting thus toward a woman who initially commanded our full attention should not be unnatural or difficult. Opening to a female fully in this way creates a wider and deeper field of arousal. In this context, sexual impulses arise out of an established, yet ever-renewing, current of love that is always dancing between partners.

To have this kind of sexual rapport, you need to be completely present, so as to take in the totality of the beauty that is there with you. There will be no multitasking at the altar of this act. If you splinter your awareness in even the slightest, most remote way at this moment, she will know it immediately. Yet if you remain fully present, being a masculine crucible for the act of lovemaking, you will see alchemical changes in her emotional and physical body. The communion will in fact alchemize the both of you on many levels.

If you are a man of integrity, you will not fail her in the act of sexual communion, for to abandon her in that hour of maximum vulnerability is to demonstrate to her what she may expect from you in all other areas of life should she remain your companion. It is a legitimate concern for a woman. If you fail to fully show up for her in moments of pleasure, how much more will you abandon her in those hours of genuine need?

Heterosexual Sexuality and Conception Potentials

The act of sex is first and foremost a procreative act, and our conscious awareness of that potential can only add to the side effects of pleasure and fulfillment while consummating sexual communion.

The capacity of married (or otherwise lifetime partnership-oriented) heterosexual couples to conceive and produce offspring carries with it an extended dimensionality with regard to sexual intercourse, due primarily to the potential for conception. The import of conception as a possibility in fertile heterosexual couples can provide an added dimensional texture in heterosexual intercourse if held consciously.

The actual choosing and accepting of an individual to mother or father one's children is about as large a gesture of personal affirmation as any one person can make to another in this life. Intentionally folding that awareness consciously into lovemaking is a profound experience and one that heterosexual couples should cherish since it is available to them.

This understanding is not meant to diminish or lessen the lovemaking value of homosexual couples (or to any couples who cannot conceive children), but simply to bring to light a very precious opportunity for life partners with conception potential not to miss.

Such couples' sexual consummation can create a refined energetic field around the act of sexual communion that permeates the moment of conception when a new being is being invoked into physical embodiment. The energetic quality of the parents at conception has profound life-contributing effects on the child that cannot necessarily be articulated, but nonetheless are present. Awareness fields around the conceiving parents form critical aspects of the physiological environment that affect conception. Like all other creative equations in the phenomenal universe, subtle and unseen energies constitute the principal influence regarding the outcomes of unfolding manifestation.

Swinging and Polygamy

When a woman opens her heart to a man, she quite organically opens to one, and not many. Her selection process includes not just a shoring up of a suitable father for progeny and protection, but also includes considerations of a lifelong pair bond that meets a deeply seated emotional rapport need.

The choice of a man of quality ensures that her gifting over of her feminine potency will serve her a lifetime and not be wasted on unreliable men who will abandon her after many years as she has moves through the triple goddess journey of maiden, mother and elder matriarch.

Any man's desire to bring "third party" intrusions into a couple's sacred sexual intimacy will more than likely be an initiation based on his own self-serving desires and not his partner's. The action can rarely be considered much more than titillation-based eroticism.

A partnered woman may be open to the act as a gesture of love and/or submission to her male lover's desires, but it is rare indeed that a woman actually craves another male or female lover when she feels complete in her primary relationship, and the same goes for a man.

On a purely energetic level, the introduction of foreign male energy into the sexual proximity of a bonded female will more than likely have an eroding effect on her primary bond. The act can have a devastating effect on the sense of safety and trust she places in her man's capacity to protect her from radiance depletion.

A woman sees her ability to captivate and satisfy her lover's whole attention as a sign that she is cherished and desired above all others by her lover. His allowing her body to be handled and entered by another man is a core violation of an unspoken creed of fidelity in the sexual pair bonding of humans. If she is compelled by her beloved to give away something her own heart would certainly choose to contain as sacred only for her man, then in the moment of that third-party act, something may be forever lost that cannot be retrieved.

Polygamists actually impose a structure of multiple-party intimacy that prohibits any ability for coherent sexual pair bonding. No woman can feel held above all others if she is merely rotated in, on occasion, to the bed of her husband. Polygamy is a distorted male control paradigm in one of its most flagrant forms and has no place in authentic core masculine expression.

Pornography

Look closely at pornography and you will see the same thing acted out over and over. It is the reduction of the masculine and feminine roles into shadow forms. Pornography is in fact the physical act of sex without the essential human connection.

For the masculine part, the natural masculine expression of initiative, leadership, celebration, protection and virility in pornography devolves into dominance, control, humiliation and a false sense of conceptualized potency.

For the woman, her natural sense of surrender, receptivity and wild-natured abandon sinks to the baser acts of demonstrative performances designed to please the "male voyeurs" she imagines are watching. For the woman engaged in pornography, these are literally sexual performances that are fueled by her unbalanced need and dependency for male approval and attention. The sexual acts themselves usually mean little to her though she will act as though they do to capture the male audience.

The mutual exploitation here is simply a dance of tragic codependency. It is in fact rather ironic to discover that both the male and female role players in pornography think they have "power" over the other.

Women engaging in pornography feel they have power over a man's desires and can captivate him with their physical allure and adventuresome acts. A woman in this role often can't believe that men actually pay to simply see her display herself and or to have sex. She perceives men who would fork over money just to simply watch her act sexually as "easily had."

The men who make and watch porno films are often astonished that women "actually do" what they ask them to do when they pay them money to do it. They think they have power over the women because they can get them to do their sexual bidding just for money.

Men in the midst of pornographic production get off on the power trip, but for the women involved it's different. Women simply utilize their participation in pornography to acquire something outside of it. Those "somethings" may be money and material things, status, security, attention and/or fame.

Men may make money by making pornography, but for them there is also an inherent pathological collusion involved in the act of creating it that is absent for women. Men get intoxicated by the act of pornography, whereas women often prefer to get intoxicated literally with drugs or alcohol to perform the act of pornography so that they don't have to feel the profane nature of sex without love.

Men want to feel potency, women want to feel connection, and pornography is the fast-food version of both because it may appear fulfilling on these counts but it's substantively empty. Pornography, like any other flawed attempt at meeting genuine human needs, will in the end squander vital time and energy on action that does not revitalize, does not re-energize. It is by nature a dead-end street, a non sequitur of disillusioned physical expression.

Paying for
Sexual Favor

They say that prostitution is the world's oldest profession, and there may be good reason for it. As long as men fail to integrate their true masculine core, cavalier versions of sexual activity will always be around. Making the act of buying sexual favor illegal has driven this historical activity into dark, desperate and dangerous corners. Without necessarily condoning the activity, it is clear to me that legislative bodies have generated a toxic criminal environment around the sexual entertainment industry that has become a greater danger to public health and safety then if those laws had instead been written to regulate rather than criminalize the activity.

Whether it is a high-end escort, a stripper showgirl or a sensual massage provider, purchasing sexual favor has a long history and is no passing fad. Men who fail to achieve a necessary self-intimacy will struggle with establishing a full and complete connection with their primary relationships, and the consequence will usually lead to straying sexual appetites that are superficial and temporary.

Prostitution is a way for men to extract base sexual experiences by simply purchasing them. By reducing the encounter to a business transaction, it takes it to a place that unrealized men are comfortable with. The parameters are defined, the superficial exchange is predictable and the post-sex residual complications are hopefully reduced to a "thank you" and "goodbye." Until men can learn to occupy their own masculine core, a good majority will seek out these kinds of dalliances if they are available to them.

"Spiritualized" sex workers provide a little fiber to the greasy cheeseburger that is known as prostitution here in America. Many of these so-called "goddess" sex workers, or "tantrikas" as they often call themselves here in the U.S., are well-intentioned, but unfortunately misguided. They purport to inject some kind of spiritual integrity into sex work. Even though charging for sexual favor cannot graduate far beyond adult entertainment, still tantrikas somehow see themselves as conducting some soulfully sanctified ritual of deep spiritual significance when they charge for their sexual services. It may indeed be true that for many men the candle-and-incense-laden experience of tantrika prostitution may be a nicer-smelling and nicer-feeling one. It may allow for some men a sense that prostitution can be not only guilt-free but also maybe even good for one as well.

Letting a woman fully dictate the terms of a sexual encounter might be oddly therapeutic for some men who have control pathologies or who have never thought of a woman as anything much more than an object to be controlled. However, the mutual usery of the business encounter hardly suggests much capacity for healthy sexual exchange. The tantrika sales pitch suggests that a woman can sexually initiate a man into some sort of kundalini(chakra energy)-driven spiritual epiphany that will assist him into discovering his core masculinity. The fact is that no woman can ever initiate a man into his core. This is a man's own responsibility.

Today, popular proponents of "good sex" like to use catchy phrases like "sacred sexuality," touting a kind of high-minded concept sex, and perhaps linking it to purported spiritual maxims. They advocate for sexual techniques that enhance "performance" and pleasure. They suggest esoteric practices such as semen retention, breathing structures, the channeling of orgasmic energy up the spine and willful control of arousal dynamics. Yet the focus is still on physiology and male paradigm impositions of textbook will and control, when so much of what is beautiful about sexuality is our surrender to the nature of its fluid and unrestrained spontaneity.

In the final analysis, paying for sexual favor or employing high-concept sexuality tactics for men will never amount to any profound sense of deeper self-intimacy, no matter how many candles are involved and no matter what the rhetoric promises. For men, prostitution and sexual entertainment in particular will always be simply what they have been from the beginning, sophomoric relief from basic male tensions that are designed to accommodate those who lack the skill to integrate a full masculine sexual refinement into their core expression as men.

Older and Younger Women

As I age I notice I am attracted to bond with women my own age, and there is less of a draw to pair-bond with younger women, as the myth about men goes. It's not that I don't find youthful women beautiful, of course, it's just that there is generally not the kind of deep attraction I desire to partner with because the depth of rapport just isn't what it is with women my own age.

Rapport is significant to the chemistry of attraction. It is also significant to sexuality. Attraction that includes real rapport beyond physicality is something I call depth attraction. Women are hard on themselves as they age, and it is understandable because the media culture values and emphasizes youthful looks. But the truth is that a mature man in his realized core will generally require the depth of beauty that only women of compatible years can provide, if he wishes to have full rapport in his sexuality.

For a man in his middle years, sex with a much younger woman is typically a fractional experience. Depth attraction is essential for any complete sexual experience. Women of mature age who can provide rapport at that depth ought not to discount that virtue and dismiss themselves and their beauty by comparing their skin and body tone to young women and girls.

As mature men, we naturally crave mature women. How delightful to look into a woman's eyes and know you are connecting with someone who has seen as many days as you have on this planet and to see how beautifully she has aged on her journey. The hype of youth is way oversold. As mature men, we ought to celebrate our own advancing years and the corresponding beauty of our age-equivalent sisters.

14

Consciousness, Intelligence and Education

Facts are all we are giving
Dissecting life instead of living
Tampering with truth until it lies.

— From *Ologies and Isms*

Education, Knowledge and Information

Men have always had a love affair with knowledge. If that knowledge is time-tested in service to our culture, it graduates to wisdom and is handed down to our children as such. Yet much of what our culture regards as knowledge today is really just the exposure to and retrieval of static information that positions itself as a myriad of titillating dry factoids that have no life in them. These days, wisdom is fading by degree, and fading fast. On the internet, speed and volume produce info-bytes that are churned out daily for the masses, like McDonald's hamburgers. We are fed drive-through ideas and opinions that are conjured up so fast that the lack of deliberation and consideration in them leaves us feeling bloated with a kind of hyper-conceptual indigestion. Men have lost the craft of retaining, conveying and generating true knowledge, and our culture limps along reflecting that sad reality.

Education itself appears less concerned about accessing authentic and inspired original content, favoring instead an emphasis on the memorization and regurgitation of already-existing bodies of information. Read through much of today's graduate school thesis writing and it reveals very little original thinking and reads much more like the veritable re-slinging of old hash, maybe with a slight twist and a fresh title. But reorganizing dead bodies of information into fresh-looking packages is more the work of morticians than it is the work of dynamic scholars. The current academic process makes education more a synonym for indoctrination into static thinking.

Because of the nature and emphasis of the prevailing academic environment, there is very little vision in the work and business affairs of the men who are the alumni of dimensionless education. Vision may in fact not be emphasized in educational institutions because evaluating it in students requires instructors and administrations who themselves embody the capacity for vision and wisdom. Furthermore, without wise academic instruction, inspired and intuitive intelligence in students will often be misinterpreted as esoteric or perhaps even in the realm of the mystical or occult—inappropriate content that appears cumbersome when referenced and examined through traditional academic review.

If a brilliant insight has no scholastically accepted precedent, or is so far from the mainstream mode of thinking and acting that its novelty begins to exceed the culturally excepted standards of appropriate innovation, it can be easily brushed aside as unfounded, reckless, too radical or even mad. Status quo is king in static academic environments and innovators can be the lunatic fringe until, for whatever reason, their genius gains traction in mainstream thoroughfares.

True education will require a kind of scholastic renovation at the gates of all established educational protocol. The goals inherent in instructive processes ought to be similar to that seen at Olympic games, where athletes compete not just against the present field, but also against the top records that have been established there. Knowing a lot of information means being knowledgeable, but an active intelligence ought to descend on information like soldiers onto a battlefield, intent on occupying it to suit the fulfillment of a new and deeper mission.

Irrelevant information, evasive abstractions and agenda-riddled reasoning are the bane of our culture today and have become the common terrain of corrupt power brokers and common politicians. These hustlers elude a proper challenge from the common public sector because our standards for education and knowledge are not bold enough to graduate free-thinking generations that have the potency of thought and deed to dethrone flawed power paradigms.

Lateral Knowledge and Ephemeral Intelligence

Fundamentally, there are two kinds of information accessible to human beings, which I refer to as "lateral knowledge" and "ephemeral intelligence."

Lateral knowledge is information that has already "landed" amid the realm of human understanding and is moving about from one "station" or person to the next. Lateral knowledge moves among people through the framework of time and memory. Perceptions that are consistently recognized and traditionally accepted as reliable become uniformly applicable to mainstream thought and incorporated into the language. Lateral knowledge is pressed into play mostly through our educational institutions, cultural influences and language paradigms.

Ephemeral intelligence is wholly different. It is not static, has not necessarily existed prior and is sourced from the sublime crucible of the original One Intelligence that created the universe. Ephemeral intelligence comes through humans in moments that are often described as insight, inspiration, intuition, or flashes of brilliance and creative genius.

Einstein's theory of $E=mc^2$ was a product of ephemeral intelligence. Until that inspired moment, that equation existed only in the realm of the One Intelligence and had not collapsed into the reality and experience of human lateral knowledge.

Men who are fully coherent in their masculine core are able to access ephemeral intelligence as easily as common men utilize lateral knowledge. Men who are able to access and express both lateral and ephemeral intelligence make very potent masculine expressions in the world because they combine a fluid creative capacity with a grounded practicality that can carry an abundance of insights to fruition efficiently.

The "Chalice Effect"

The ability to receive ephemeral intelligence is not limited to age or even IQ. Insight and brilliance are available to anyone at any time. However, the capacity to process and integrate ephemeral intelligence into the functioning and cellular experiences of an individual correlates with time and age. If we were to see the bowl of a v-shaped chalice as our capacity to integrate ephemeral intelligence, with youth at its narrow end and old age at the rim, we would see how the expanding shape increases with time, increasing the holding capacity of mature understandings as we approach old age.

In fact, the capacity for the deepest and most accurate understandings and expression of wisdom regarding the human condition can be felt in a healthy, still-active mind, when the influence of the event horizon of death is imminent and can be sensed in the individual as an intimate proximity, and not just an abstraction of things to come.

There is a saying, "youth is wasted on the young." The statement reflects the common frustration mature adults feel as their bodies decline and their capacity for retention and integration of wisdom increases. There are very rare cases of individuals who experience a complete liberation of the subjective self (through early-life deconstruction) that allows for absolute integration at relatively young ages, such as in the case of The Buddha or Jesus. But generally most men require a journey to at least midlife before the "chalice bowl" really begins to widen so that significant content can be retained.

My first mentor was a woman named Alice Simms who was 76 years old when I met her. I was a very inquisitive 16-year-old. She used to tell me often, in regard to certain teachings, "You're not ready for that." In spite of my youthfully exuberant protests pleading with her to share certain instruction or spiritual materials with me she would be resolute and firm in her boundaries. Any ritually conducted rights of passage for young men, and indeed, any emerging adults, must be limited in their scope and intent to the developmentally appropriate content suitable for that age. Useful instruction should assist them in evolving to the next level of their lives, rather than trying to stuff all of life's complex and nuanced intricacies into a young mind that cannot possibly wrap itself around the material it's being exposed to.

Consciousness

It is significant to consider that so much emphasis has been placed on the physical evolution of the human being and very little, if any, credence given to the evolution of consciousness that has unfolded within human expression and action since our primal ancestors started this journey. Valuing the quality of individual consciousness means placing worth on a human quality that is not susceptible to distinction by virtue of race, gender, color, ethnicity or religion, because consciousness itself is not a product of genetic selection (though it may be influenced by it).

We have assumed by some kind of default reasoning that DNA and not consciousness itself is responsible for how great a person is. History has clearly shown the absolute error in this line of thinking. Most rulers who have come to power as a result of a direct lineage to great leaders have, as offspring, been somewhere between mediocre and tragically flawed. Yet we continue even today with family lineages that, following the death of the ruling parent, put the next generation at the helm as national leaders.

That is why I emphasize in this book that our attention ought to be where universal and lasting change can take place, that being the seat of human consciousness itself as embodied by every particular individual. We will not make better men by breeding some "master race" of genetically idealized specimens; we will make better men by studying and teaching the art of embodying consciousness.

Running the field of localized awareness that some might call a soul through the instrument of the human body is in fact where the art of living skillfully primarily occurs. Utilizing the entire multidimensional nature of the awareness matrix within each human being requires a rarely embodied scope of understanding that moves readily and fluidly between the cognitive and the intuitive.

Our individual consciousness is intimately wedded to a field of impersonal awareness that ultimately unfolds from the over-arching presence of the Godhead. This Trinity of sublime sentience is ours to reconcile, as the evolution of the human condition requires. The prevailing consciousness paradigms of men however, remain fixated on the limiting field of the personal awareness dimension only. Like a bug splat on the windshield, we as men have become preoccupied with a speck of insect guts on the glass surface while we miss the resplendent panoramic view before us.

Spirit is not limited to the animation of body and thought. Being solely occupied as a person with the surface animations of the physical body and the subjective persona is the error most humans make in the act of participating in their own existence. We fail often to recognize that most of the iceberg is under the water.

Indeed, the composite of total activation within the full dimension of subjective presence in human beings runs straight through to the Creator itself, seamlessly and uninterrupted. Our legacy as self-aware beings in the universe has very few limitations when fully actualized. Were it not for the event horizon around the point of singularity of intimacy, we might actually survive the subjective journey intact into the heart of God. By design, our total apprehension of the Creator remains gracefully irreconcilable, but not much else, it seems, is out of reach.

In the new order, the old maxim changes. Space is not the last frontier; consciousness will be the final frontier for humans. Spaceships will not take us to the center of our experience as sentient beings; consciousness is the vehicle we must skillfully maneuver deep into the heart of life to make the ultimate discoveries regarding the full potential of our own existence.

Instruction and Transmission

When I was a young man I was hungry for authentic teachers who would help me discover how to be a fully realized person. I remember finding books that I felt were quite inspiring reads, and then feeling stunningly disappointed when I finally met the author in person for a talk or lecture. I was genuinely surprised to find out that more often than not the author was in many ways not walking the talk.

At some point an older friend of mine, referring to the controversial Bhagwan Shree Rashneesh, jokingly counseled me. "Robert, never confuse the messenger with the message," he said laughingly. For me it was not an amusing statement. I didn't just want inspired words to read, I wanted a living teacher who embodied his or her inspired words. I understood intuitively that I wanted and needed transmission of wisdom from embodied sources, not spiritually pedantic treatises on trendy self-awareness themes.

Even if an inspired book can serve to be a helpful instruction manual toward a clarity of being, nothing can replace the direct transmission of authors who have embodied their words in deed. Personal, direct transmission from teacher to student is an alchemical medicine that cannot be substituted.

Authentic instruction in the art of embodying human awareness is very, very hard to come by. Very few people in history have marshaled a working mastery over the craft of consciousness, let alone taken up a position of offering instruction regarding it, and when they do, it is as if they are always speaking about the subject in parables or metaphor. Speaking about something that must be directly experienced to be truly known is an art in itself. When it comes to something as intimate as the nature of each individual's consciousness and his or her particular relationship to life, it is very difficult to speak concretely about any part of it as absolute.

Human instruments who are adept at embodying consciousness become, as beings, abhorrent to category, definition or replication. This makes any legitimate instruction in consciousness by them dependent upon a living transmission from them while they are still alive. No transmittable teaching that is profoundly effective regarding the nature of consciousness can occur from outside a direct experience with the actual embodied source of that level of attainment. This is why many ancient cultures valued the student-disciple relationship.

Religion and spirituality have tried to corner the market on the art of living coherently. Science has no interest in what it cannot control and measure, and oligarchies have no interest in what they cannot profit from. Religion and spirituality have stepped in to claim a proprietary interest in the mystical domain of the posthumous esoteric teachings of the few liberated souls who have come and gone.

But religion, and to a large degree spirituality, are not sufficient to the task of awakening the dormant soul. To have change in the masculine today, we need direct transmission from authentically embodied men who have excelled at the art of expressing consciousness. It is not enough to channel inspired material without a proper embodiment of that knowledge. Channels and vessels of gifted insights were the teachers of past eras. The new order requires an actual embodiment to facilitate the necessary evolution. These are men who reveal a demonstrative presence that seamlessly represents the teaching they offer. Learning from books may trigger conceptual understanding, but embodied presence can effect direct transmission.

Human Potentials in Consciousness

Much of the contemporary male-influenced spirituality within the last 50 years has suggested that there is some form of spiritual mastery, attainment, enlightenment, nirvana or conscious awakening that will bring us to a point of divine perfection, an apotheosis where our awareness will have arrived at some permanent and fully liberated state of being. It is a seductive promise, and one that is misleading.

Running consciousness through the human instrument is an art form, yet even that craft has its limitations—we cannot become gods when we are merely reflections of the Divine. The restriction is inherent because we are by nature the created and not the Creator. We exist within the unfolding dream of the ineffable Creator as objects within the phenomenal matrix, and no one can fully apprehend the dream from inside the dream—and because we as bodies become points of subjective experience, we are stuck inside the dream. Our greatest potential for any sort of liberation from the dream state is remaining ever aware of the nature of the dream while existing within the dream itself; this reveals itself as a self-reflexive quality similar to what one experiences when lucidly dreaming.

The particular heightened state of awareness we are capable of expressing as humans is as sublime as it is profound, yet it is hardly omniscient. Historical figures such as Christ, Buddha and Krishna arise periodically throughout history to give testimony to the potentials of human consciousness embodiment, and they do so by revealing the capacity of human presence to penetrate through the veil of the cosmic dance, and touch back directly into the Source Intelligence that is dreaming us into being. The examples they demonstrate teach us that the true path is not found in the practice of blind faith, nor is it found in some individually attained spiritual apotheosis. The greatest victory, they point out, is in the sustained lucid reconciling of the dream state in which we abide as devoted subjects animated by the imagination of God. Clarity within the dream state grants a grace-governed access to streams of insight from the Intelligence that created us, however that is all it grants. That being said, such a degree of conscious awareness is no small event. As relatively limited as awakened single-point consciousness may be compared to the Godhead we emerge from, our field of awareness does contain the ultimate expression of human potential, and its possibilities are absolutely magical. The purest heroic journey for men is the one that will finally reconcile and wed the dreamed with the dreamer, a sublime odyssey that will invite our complete redemption as created entities in the phenomenal universe.

COHERENT AND INCOHERENT
MASCULINE MODELS

He ends the war of millions
And begins the Reign of One
And no armor will protect him
For no sorrows will he shun.

— From *I Shall Fight No More Forever*

Searching for Mr. Right

Human beings are not perfect, and this book is not about the realization of perfect men. It is certainly sufficient enough to have men who are, on balance, into their core expression and demonstrating coherent male activation as a relatively consistent movement. It is essential to have living examples of the actualized masculine, but for the written medium of a book, being able to cite and discuss historical ones can be helpful.

I will, for our purposes, cite three remarkable American examples of integrated masculine embodiment: martial arts grand master Bruce Lee, President Abraham Lincoln and non-violence practitioner Martin Luther King, Jr. Each in his own way and through his own personal style displays a degree of core masculine realization that is both revealing and inspiring. Rather than levy complete biographies, I will focus on the unique characteristics that I believe set them free into a realized expression of their core masculine.

The Case of Bruce Lee

Ask anyone who ever sparred with the late martial arts iconoclast Bruce Lee and they will all tell you the same thing: yes, he was fast, remarkably intelligent, skilled and fierce, certainly a superb physical specimen, but most striking of all, they will say, was his uncanny capacity to anticipate his opponent.

Everyone who fought with Lee says his timing was extraordinary, giving one the sense that he was reading the mind of his opponent. But Lee was no mind reader. Lee had great timing because he absorbed his opponent. Lee understood that martial combat came down to the art of relationship. His expression of martial response in combat situations came directly from his attunement to the relationship he was establishing with his opponent. But the most fundamental relationship Lee developed, the one that allowed him to raise his art to mastery, was the relationship he had with himself.

Lee's book, *Tao of Jeet Kune Do*, reveals his revelations on the matter. One of the master hand-to-hand combat warriors of our age, Lee had discovered within himself the fine art of sublimating to the feminine. The balanced teachings of the Tao had most certainly pointed him in the proper direction, but however it occurred to him, it is obvious that Lee had realized the masculine core through a keen integration of the feminine into his emphasized masculine core.

In his fierce desire for martial excellence, Lee left no stone unturned, and his search pressed him well outside of the traditional combat techniques he initially studied. Traditional Wing Chun may have provided a young Lee with a platform to work from, but the static doctrine and limited Kung Fu forms would ultimately not suffice for Lee as he deconstructed and incorporated the feminine in pursuit of excellence. Kung Fu as a pure tradition eventually mirrored for Lee the structured morbidity of masculine force (control) without fluid feminine integration (instinct), and Lee hungered for full martial expression.

As a result Lee branched out and created his own form of martial art, Jeet Kun Do (JKD). Drawing on the philosophy of the Tao, JKD integrated a fluid, open style of fighting in which coherent understanding of and relationship with the opponent were key components in reaching an excellence in martial execution in combat.

Physical conditioning was critical, as were discipline and skill, but what became essential to Lee to achieve his extraordinary success as a fighting champion was his refined and uniquely cultivated state of awareness. Beyond his formidable application of personal will, Lee had discovered the art of surrender to the fluid intuitive. In the opening pages of his book, Lee states, "The consciousness of self is the greatest hindrance to the proper execution of all physical action."

The self-absorbed subjective paradigm can never achieve extraordinary excellence of expression while confined to its own limited awareness field, and Lee understood this absolutely. Elements of his journey of deconstruction seem to have occurred during an extended convalescence when he was recovering from a serious back injury in 1970. It was during this time that he wrote volumes of notes that would posthumously comprise *The Tao of Jeet Kun Do*.

For Lee, natural flow and balance internally translated to an optimally fierce expression externally that would explode upon an opponent with searing intensity. What is most noticeable about Lee's fighting style is not just his fine execution of action, but also his incredible capacity for restraint. Lee learned to "listen" to his opponent in much the same way Muhammad Ali would do in the opening rounds before launching a blistering offensive later on in the match. Listening and openness are just a couple of examples of the many feminine archetypal attributes that most men miss on their way to excellence of expression. Lee represents a fine example of the fierce masculine refined and enhanced by feminine integration in the post-deconstruction phase—a remarkable achievement for a man to realize in his late twenties.

The Case of Abraham Lincoln

Men move only by the grace of God, and no one understood this more intensely than our 16th president, Abraham Lincoln. What made Lincoln such an icon of executive strength and leadership was, ironically, his humility and abiding sense of ongoing surrender to the greater uncertainties of life. In the face of an abomination most of us could barely comprehend, Lincoln stood undaunted by his task as if sentenced by a higher power to the hellish term he faced. Lincoln confirmed and consecrated himself to an inglorious (in his lifetime) mission that would elicit a particularly debilitating suffering to his heart so grave and soul-wrenching that no one on earth could appreciably soothe or comfort it.

Lincoln affects us so deeply today primarily because of his capacity to endure the very intimate relationship he would establish between his own deeply responsive sensibilities and the raw outward realities he faced in his lifetime. Known to have been plagued all his life by a recurring melancholy, Lincoln had an ability to allow for, and coexist with, the disturbing aspects of his own complex, sensitive nature that mirrored his capacity to endure the complicated external tribulations of the nation surrounding his service during his presidency.

Lincoln's leadership to his country is a clear and compelling example of a man who had sublimated his masculine power through the humbling fires of the terrible feminine. His presidency became the crucible of his descent into ashes. Arising out from this trial by fire, Lincoln was able to navigate the country through a wrenchingly devastating civil war with grace, authority and wisdom, becoming arguably the most profound example of presidential leadership this country has ever known.

The Case of Martin Luther King, Jr.

The compellingly raw power of nonviolence may be one of the most underestimated forces ever displayed in the human social arena. It is a power capable of dispelling an occupying empire or establishing civil rights where embedded hatred and ignorance once forged the laws. The potency of Gandhi's version of Ahimsa nonviolence represents an example of masculine ferocity when the feminine is fully integrated in with it. The nonviolence of Martin Luther King, Jr., and Mahatma Gandhi married restraint with ferocity, humility with determination, acceptance with defiance—in essence, the masculine with the feminine.

Many mistake nonviolence as a lifestyle. But nonviolence was never presented by King as primarily a universal lifestyle; it was for him fundamentally an instrument of change. He understood well that the process of nonviolence would become, for his cause, a creative device of social leveraging that could be utilized in an environment where social conscience was woven into the existing cultural paradigm.

The fact that nonviolence has worked in America bodes well as a testimony to the conscience at work within our traditional heritage as a people. Nonviolence would never have worked in Saddam Hussein's Iraq or Hitler's Nazi Germany. Both King and Gandhi would have swiftly been made brutal examples of what happens to those who embody dissention in the face of totalitarian regimes. But King boldly demonstrated the power and potential that feminine integration can have when injected into the American social fabric where the values of freedom, liberty and equality are perpetual cultural axioms.

King, the man, like Gandhi before him, was not just some "nice guy" passively pleading for change. He was a bold and passionate example of a man in his true masculine core, intensely dedicated to a beautiful vision of the human condition well beyond his time. After centuries of human slavery in one form or another, King arose from his ancestry, not blind with rage, but victoriously, bearing a calculated masculine ferocity designed to shatter the tyranny of old ways with a redeeming vision of the human heart so compelling that change seemed inevitable.

The force of those changes was intimately wedded to the fluid and transforming power of the feminine that King would illicit through the instrument of nonviolence. He did not personally bring Jim Crow to its knees, ultimately the conscience of the American people at large did. The genius of King was his capacity for direct, unflinching action, combined with stalwart humility and surrender to a vision and fate he trusted implicitly. In the face of a culturally localized dark abomination, he stood firmly rooted in his masculine actualization. His dream was not mitigated even by the recognition of his own limitations as a mortal instrument. His soul soared above the flesh, and his hope would restructure the social conscience of America.

King put the oppression and subjugation of the black experience in the south of the 1960s into full view and into American living rooms across the country through the medium of television news. Images of decent, law-abiding American citizens of various colors getting beaten by police and hosed down by firemen in the streets were more than the conscience of the nation could stomach. Civil rights legislation was the culture's response to King's leadership in the arena of racial equality, a movement whose potency was derived directly from King's natural affinity toward feminine integration, which was in turn transformed into benevolent masculine action.

Qualities and Virtues

Along with historical examples of coherent masculine embodiment, it is helpful to cite certain qualities of expression that are themselves facets of core masculine integration. It is simplistic and unwise to assume that some static written standard, or code of conduct, will suffice as a complete educational instrument for the fully coherent functioning and expression of the masculine. However, I like to think of the virtues listed below as a skeletal framework upon which may be hung the flesh of a living benevolent action in the world.

Initiation: The quality that begins necessary action without requiring prompting, inviting, requesting or affirming.

Compassion: Allowing for and lending a caring credence to the perceived reality of another.

Patience: The ability to allow for and respond with the organic pace and rhythm of life.

Humility: The capacity to allow for the natural course of events to unfold without resistance to it, and to participate fully in life without attempting to impose personal control on any part of it.

Tenderness: A profound emotional reverence that elicits a soft-hearted sentiment toward the object of attention.

Passion: The full activation of one's individual talents and gifts to express one's heartfelt integrity.

Wisdom: The application of the faculties of listening to Core Intelligence.

Power: The capacity to bring to bear the unmitigated life force within a particular person.

Fierceness: The bold expression of authentic power.

Integrity: The genuine and accurate expression of what is sensed to be true; a loyalty to the current of life.

Sacrifice: The inherent instinct to boldly serve life without compromise, even unto death.

Courage: The capacity to perform when it is essential to perform, no matter what, even unto death.

Protectiveness: The inherent instinct and capacity to provide for the safety and well-being of one's family and community, as well as the natural environment one habituates.

Mirth: The tendency toward an organic expression of benevolent humor and play that celebrates life.

The Dark Side

Understanding where the masculine goes bad is as important as knowing how it expresses itself coherently. Extreme cases are useful to highlight, and in this chapter I will discuss three individuals who corrupted the masculine in a devastatingly destructive way: Adolph Hitler, Jim Jones and Charles Manson. The nature, depth and historical impact of these individuals ought not to be overlooked in any serious discussion of how and why the masculine can go so dangerously wrong.

These individuals are stark examples of the risk and danger inherent in the masculine expression when it is not grounded in and integrated with the feminine and proceeds to career forth with intense energy toward exponentially greater and greater distortion. Initial fragmentations in the awareness field of young men can prove to be dangerously vulnerable to dark influences in subtler realms that become drawn to the discordant energy and attach. Protecting our youth through a positive community, coherent adult male role models, and appropriate ritualized rites of passage is essential to safeguard against these kinds of extreme cases of masculine deformation.

It is interesting to note that while each of these men is a very dark historical figure, they all exhibited as younger men exceptionally intelligent, creative and charismatic personas. Each one also demonstrated an extraordinary capacity for leadership. These attributes, it is worth noting, are some key markers for core masculine expression in general, however as we will see in these particular cases, the masculine center of these men was severely broken, while a morbidly contrived shadow masculine persona gained momentum over their lifetime.

Adolph Hitler:
Exploiting Cultural Distortion

Modern historians have little trouble with the current interpretation that Hitler's dark ambition was driven to some extent by the trauma he experienced in the German trenches of WWI. But prior to that, as a young man Adolph Hitler was an aspiring artist. Hitler's pragmatic father rebuked him for pursuing such an unproductive career interest and forced him into studies that would lead to a more legitimate (i.e., financially responsible) career path.

But Hitler's artistic affinities were not merely products of a passing youthful fancy; they were soulfully ingrained aptitudes that passionately yearned for expression. The artistic repression of his formative years failed to mute Hitler's fevered energy, however, and what was perhaps a potentially coherent expression became redirected into a brutal landscape of political ambition.

In order to burn brightly, Hitler would soak the rags of his tattered soul in the kerosene of a particularly maniacal ambition. His ruthless rise to political power was paralleled by a toxic and morbid isolation that increased over time, feeding an already radical paranoia.

The rage inside Hitler was marked and noteworthy. His anger, clearly visible in almost all of his speeches, is driven by the core disconnect between himself and life, and he assigned blame and put to death innocent people by the millions in a grotesque attempt to assuage his inner distortions.

Hitler succeeded in inflicting so much devastation because aspects of his defective persona were mirrored in the culture he influenced. The schism that confounded Germany's post-WWI nationalism created a disconnect between the government of reparation and the people who drove it. By the time Hitler was at the zenith of his power, when the corruption and insanity of his reign had made itself glaringly apparent, it became difficult for anyone in the country to simply opt out, and there was no one inside the German war machine who was able to stop the momentum of the Reich.

What is important to understand in the case of Hitler is that when cultures are broken they are vulnerable to flawed masculine leadership that reflects that distortion. Tyrants are particularly adept at exploiting the social wounds of the people they rule. The people of the nation are like the immune system of the body—when they are weak, broken and tired, they are more susceptible to hosting a disease/despot that can overrun and destroy them.

Jim Jones: Messianic Mania

Jim Jones' ascension to power came through the ironic cloak of church ministry, which he utilized to gain social power. Upon examination, the life of Jim Jones reflects a confused mix of seemingly honorable intentions initially, which gradually began to mutate into a perverted and intense personal agenda that crescendoed in a lethal messianic complex that left hundreds dead in Jones' jungle compound in Guyana.

The interior demons that plagued Jones all his life fused his persona to the dark wounds that comprised his early life. His life became, by degree, an increasingly malevolent maelstrom of distortion that deepened without deviation toward its inevitable destruction. Feigning authentic power, he utilized masculine-appearing qualities in an emphatic display of maniacal tyranny that his followers believed were about paternal protection and guidance. His dramatic fervor, intensity and mock authority captivated a smoldering idealism within his devotees that galvanized their commitment to him.

Jones seemed to know just what to say, when to say it and how to deliver it. Like a charming serpent he slithered his way into the local political scenes of the day, rubbing elbows with those in high office and touting grand ideas of liberating the poor and the oppressed.

Jones was skilled at manipulating those around him, but like all false men, his lack of integrity toward authentic masculine integration resulted in a pitiful and inevitable personal failure, which ultimately led to the demise of hundreds of those who had put faith in his twisted utopian vision.

Like Hitler, Jones' acerbic scrutiny of the social structures he rose from led him finally to an isolated compound where his dictatorial ideology would rule with an iron fist. In the Guyana jungle compound, Jones attempted to fuse his devoted followers to his own demented paternal vision, while proclaiming the outside social orders he condemned as corrupt. Like Hitler he would die by his own hand as the outside world encroached upon his disintegrating reign.

Charles Manson: The Wounded Dealer

The scope of Manson's destruction with regard to the sheer numbers of lives lost may be less than either Hitler or Jones, but the intimacy of his deception and manipulation of those few he influenced to do his bidding are graphically revealing. With regard to the women he convinced to perform unspeakable acts of depravity, what reveals itself is an intimate view into what occurs when a deeply distorted feminine couples with a dangerously derailed masculine.

Manson himself is neither physically nor intellectually imposing. He, in fact, sent others to carry out his wicked instructions. His intrigue comes with the particular way he negotiated his significant personal pain. The fragmented echoes of his original wounds are revealed even today in his unending rhetoric about his personal sense of social disconnect, distrust and disdain for the corrupt world he sees around him. He has reconciled his life's transgressions through a psychotic distortion that allows him to posture himself as the perpetually quintessential victim of an insane world.

If he were a man who had committed no crime, he might well illicit sympathy. His ongoing tirades about systemic social flaw, while distorted and perhaps quite off the mark, reflect an odd emphasis on needs that sound like justice, equality, dignity and truth—quite legitimate values common to all people.

This was the seduction of the younger Charles Manson. The depth and scope of his personal wounds from youth made a dramatic urgency out of legitimate needs that became more and more distorted the older he became. For his small band of followers, the shared sense of outrage and alienation from the social conventions of the day bound them to Manson's sophomoric messianic complex. The growing schism within Manson's own core disconnect allowed him to justify radical delusions and devious strategies that grew steadily more and more extreme until eventually the horrific happened.

It is easy to dehumanize Manson, to make a monster out of him and exile him from the rest of humanity. But Manson is no monster; he is a very damaged human being who was a party to deplorable acts. We may justifiably condemn him, but we must not avert our gaze from his grotesque error. He is, for our culture, an urgent reminder that

211

masculine coherency and a social structure that endorses it are critical on so many levels.

To Manson the world was a black-and-white affair where he was right and the rest of the world was some "thing" he could condemn and order deplorable acts against. He could justify it by severing himself from the "objects" of humanity he held in contempt, seeing himself as something somehow apart and righteous. Crimes against humanity come easy to such men because they view the world as a flawed object where violence seems almost justifiable and necessary to reconcile deep personal pain.

It would perhaps be easier on some level to digest if Charles Manson and the hideous acts he participated in were actually isolated and freakish anomalies of the human condition. But as much as we would like to believe that, can we really afford to as a society? For if we blame only Manson for the error of Manson, do we not indulge then in the same fundamental disconnect as a community that he did as an individual? Are we not led then to the same propensity of error by seeing him only as an evil object existing somehow outside the human condition, worthy of only enough consideration as to imagine what form of punitive retribution we would wish to inflict on him? Doesn't this merely mirror Manson's own pathology?

The masculine error is something we as men must all account for. For every sick brother, we must acknowledge a weak link in the overall fraternal chain. If we are ever to evolve as men, we must walk as one brotherhood and not pretend that the sickest of us is somehow an alien anomaly to the masculine body.

We must assume some responsibility as men for the Mansons of the world. Only then can we fully own what is the best and worst of our condition as male agents and begin to heal what is incoherent among us as we move toward the fraternal coherency and health that is our birthright as men.

Summarizing Masculine Error

Prisons today are full of examples of the disturbing spawn of masculine error. We can write off convicts and felons as bad seeds, inherently evil men or even irredeemable monsters. Perhaps some men may be worthy of such labels. But we must all agree that they are first and foremost our lost brothers—that no matter what they have done, we cannot conveniently cleave them out of the human race, if only for the simple fact that the Creator gave rise to them as incarnate beings in human form, no less than ourselves.

The capacity to retain an acceptance of such offenders as creatures born within the human family allows us to embrace their error as one that lies within the general human condition, and that their defect is not just some alien act of isolated evil that lies well beyond the scope of the general human experience. If we are to heal, to evolve, to understand the human condition in full, we must embrace the totality of it and not shrink or turn away in disgust and dismissal from damaged men and the darker side of our natures. We do not need to condone sick behavior to allow that it occurs within our ranks, and it is not in our best interest to deny that our sickest brothers are still our brothers in the end.

In these last three examples, perhaps the most compelling similarity is the fact that each individual failed to embody the critical masculine initiatory element of service to the whole instead of service to the self. That each of these profiles in masculine distortion displays a lifelong symphony of narcissism is no casual fact. A coherent benevolent focus on the well-being of the whole by these three individuals could well have changed their conduct of leadership and, by extension, the course of human history. But each of these tragic individuals failed to surrender to the feminine axiom that we are all fundamentally connected as human beings first and foremost, and this error allowed them to destroy life with some self-endorsed, twisted sense of self-righteousness.

It is critical that the psychotic hall of mirrors that the subjective paradigm sulks through day in and day out must one day be reconciled to a fuller integration beyond the sealed membrane of the egotistic self. In one sense Hitler, Manson and Jones were never able to serve the whole because they never really realized a conscious connection to it in the first place. As they matured in years they were not able to surrender to life itself and deconstruct, because the weight of investment in their personal delusion had become unmanageably cumbersome, and for them there was no escape from the velocity of that error.

The first rule in the art of war is to understand your enemy, and if masculine error is the enemy within, we must understand its nature, not just condemn and dismiss it. For somewhere within the abomination of violence is the key to an understanding that is essential to the redemption of that error, and as long as that error exists unresolved among us in the form of our lost brothers, then none of our hands as men is completely clean.

Marks of the Beast

The following list of troubling qualities is worth reviewing. Any one or combination of these qualities could serve as a red flag indicative of dangerously incoherent masculine conditions existing within the individual expressing them. When any one of these types of actions is known to arise within ourselves, it would do us good to consider it as a crisis that deserves prompt attention.

Denial: The refusal to accept accountability and responsibility for one's own actions.

Complaining: The emphasizing of personal dissatisfaction regarding this or that repeatedly.

Preaching: Proclaiming one's own personal views as truth that should be accepted and adopted by all.

Controlling: Attempting to gain security and comfort through the subjugation of others.

Fretting: A public demonstrative exhibition of non-life-threatening fear.

Disrespect: Behavior demonstrating a blatant disregard for the dignity due all living things.

Dishonesty: Behavior that indulges anything outside of one's own core integrity.

Bullying: The use of any power-over mechanisms utilized to force compliance of another.

Accusing: Placing a judgment regarding the behavior of another as bad, wrong or unworthy.

Raging: Indulging in public displays of anger or other loss of temper and composure.

Despairing: Obsessing on negative outlooks while indulging a general mistrust of life.

Resenting: Affixing and maintaining a blaming judgment against another.

Boasting: Bragging about oneself in any self-aggrandizing way.

Gossiping: Discussing the perceived personal qualities or actions of another publicly for personal entertainment.

Blaming: Ascribing total responsibility to another for a personally undesired outcome.

16

END GAME

Already I smell the decay of you
Which began even before your death,
You gladiator of pettiness and pomp
You Caesar of smoke and ash.

— From *I Buried You*

It's a Consciousness Thing

Anthropologists now accept that there were at least 18 earlier hominid branches in the human family tree that have come and gone. These were creatures, very similar to ourselves that actually did not survive; they ultimately became extinct for one reason or another. There are no guarantees for our species. Can we, as the last remaining hominid species with our vast momentum of error, survive ourselves? It is a fair question for any one of us to ponder.

Certainly the world of human affairs seems a lot "crazier" then it did even when I was a kid. It is not, I am convinced, actually crazier; it has just become louder, more obvious and more intense. Yet the pressure of that intensity also carries with it the quintessential elements of a transforming potential that can rupture the prevailing zeitgeist and hurl us as a species over the threshold of this increasingly festering inertia and into the next phase of human consciousness evolution.

The truth is that those expressions of the human condition that seem most appalling to us actually contain the ingredients that form the recipe of redemption to the seemingly inevitable human disaster at hand. There is a momentum building inside the intense feeling of that smoldering insanity we feel that's "out there" in the world today. Human consciousness is evolving, unfolding and transforming every moment, and that "craziness" we sense in the world today comes from being immersed in the collective pool of human awareness as that communal consciousness reaches a critical mass, in lieu of reaching its breaking point.

Extraordinary growth spikes in human evolution almost always occur in fits and spurts, whether it be cultural, intellectual or even physical. Likewise, collective human consciousness dynamics express a fevered stagnation for long stretches leading up to an explosion of large-scale immediate, radical and rapid change. Human awareness systems seem to conform well to notions of "hundredth monkey"(Dr. Lyall Watson) or "morphic resonance" (Rupert Sheldrake) because those theories lend a legitimacy to exponentially dramatic and spontaneous shifts in consciousness paradigms. Even though we cannot measure it, we may accept that quantum dynamics apply to consciousness every bit as much as they do to particle physics.

It is fitting that the sea of human consciousness transcends the contained vessels that comprise reason and logic. Awareness fields function in quantum ways we can only partially track and explore scientifically. Consciousness, though real, is far too elusive to capture and analyze as a model of quantifiable phenomenon. That collective human consciousness may suddenly unfold in a manner we cannot fathom or predict then is hardly arguable. When Roger Bannister finally broke the four-minute-mile record, he broke with it the longstanding sense of limitation that it could not be done. Human limitation is a barrier imposed through living solely within conceptual frameworks, and so it becomes necessary that we explore beyond thought systems and into the deep reaches of presence itself.

We may ultimately need to cultivate a brave new mystical science, a field of study in which the blend of the intuitive and empirical can be married in an environment where the terrain of intuitive perception will be given equal credence, even where the toolbox of conceptual apprehension and scientific deliberation cannot be used to articulate any kind of traditionally comprehensive proofs. "Singularity" is the word science understands as the very threshold of its own limited capacity for further apprehension on certain matters, and in the case of the conscious evolution of human beings, there can be no empirical dissection of the full matrix of awareness dimensions to ground pure science in. That is because inherent in the human awareness field is the event horizon of the Absolute, and the inevitability of that tends to take the wind out of most pure scientific inquiry. And yet we must not be discouraged from passionately inquiring into the most intimate human domain there is—our own field of living awareness.

A masculine cluster of clear, coherent men demonstrating right now an obvious evolution of human consciousness could present enough light to absolutely ignite a morphic shift in universal human awareness, one that would mark a profound progression in the human condition that would stick. As Roger Bannister said after breaking the

4-minute mile, "The earth seemed to move with me. I found a new source of power and beauty, a source I never knew existed."

The Human Reformation

Authentic reformation of old ways will require a radically new human movement that is not itself rooted in organizational paradigms. Yet it must, at the same time, carry with it a common residue of unifying action within the entire species. In the next evolution of masculine human expression, our common bond must be more implicit than explicit. In the new order we will have to learn to allow for indirect understandings that will establish a rapport of uniform solidarity among the masses. The challenge before our age, indeed the challenge of human evolution itself, is to dispense with the lifeless, social cohesion tools of dogmatic indoctrinations and brittle, codified morality maxims, opting instead for the sublimely subjective direction of the clear human heart.

Men of an authentic light will not build churches around themselves. Their instruction is always revealed in the way they live their life. There will be no Bible or Bill of Rights for the next evolution of men who embody real freedom. The old law of men could be written and preached, but the new law of the radical masculine is *no* law at all. It is instead the absolute faith and surrender of every man to the ubiquitous and ineffable fluid discourse of the individual soul intimately married with that of the Creator itself, out of which shall unfold the Great Design.

When it comes to the human condition, change must occur one person at a time and not by state-imposed utopian agendas such as those espoused by Marx or Lenin. To the likes of such men, change coming about one individual at a time seemed wholly unreasonable. But for every misguided or out-of-step Marx there is a coherent Emerson who understood: "Adopt the pace of nature, her secret is patience."

And so each of us, one at a time, builds the quiet revolution. And as we begin to fire across the bow of old ways, we may ask ourselves: How will we keep from slipping back into just another church of static doctrine built around a freshly inspired evolution? How will this movement avoid becoming just another regime that arises from a revolution that overthrew the previous tyranny? How will this time be different from any other time in history when the old became usurped by the new, and the new became just another version of the old? The answer is rooted in faith.

We must have faith. That faith will be grounded in the understanding that life experience has saturated the human condition for so long now, and to such a degree, that we as humans are ripe for the kind of evolutionary shift in consciousness that will lead to authentic freedom.

We must have faith. A faith that sees that a world of such modern social interconnectivity now possesses the technological leverage that, in tandem with the symbiotic rapport of mass human consciousness, can bolster and drive radical paradigm shifts immediately.

We must have faith. Faith that can sense that the time is right for the coming of benevolent and powerfully wise leadership on the horizon—that these guides will be spirits who clearly answer to the call of an Intelligence greater than the mere common thinking mind of men. These select individuals will be lights whose sacredly ordained actions will serve the heart of life and bend to no selfish agenda of individual human will.

We must have faith. Faith that the most important, most essential aspect to all real change will arise from the self-affirming trust that we have the capacity within ourselves, each of us, to quicken our own souls with a call to radical integrity.

As we embark on the journey as a species that will take us to the next frontier of human evolution, we may give gratitude for the time that is at hand. We may be grateful to be alive as we approach the emergence from the darkest hours of the human condition. We may celebrate an age where so much potential and possibility exist as we approach the threshold of a radical shift in mass human awareness fields.

The Agents of Change

Since the Renaissance, much emphasis has been placed on scientific understanding and empirical teaching. The coming era will evolve to value and emphasize a skillful, living intelligence regarding the conscious embodiment of human awareness fields. Masculine teachers who understand and embody the art of running consciousness through the instrument of the human body ought to be emphasized more than teachers of any other field of study, because out of consciousness all else unfolds. These new guides will be living repositories of wisdom regarding the nature of human awareness. Indeed, they may become the salvation of the human experiment. With their influence, the tide will begin to shift, as men of all ages are drawn to their light.

Practical change at the onset will require the conversion of men who have aged sufficiently to deconstruct into the ripe phase of male coherent expression. As a growing number of men in middle age begin to understand, accept and submit to their own midlife deconstruction process, a significant portion of them will complete the journey into wholeness as men. So the new masculine emissaries will be mostly life-ripened, middle-aged men who have taken the full descent into the ashes of their being and reemerged victoriously as living testimonies to their word. In the new order of masculine evolution, what we teach we must live and what we live we must be able to offer as hope to others if they are to abandon a familiar misery for such an unfamiliar possibility of fulfillment. New leaders can no longer afford to simply "spread the word." They must *be* the word at all times and at all costs.

Deconstructed men will become the knights of a kind of prodigal reformation, as they return home from the darkness. These men will be young enough to make contributions that will still be relevant to the culture, but old enough to be grounded in their core by virtue of having passed through the crucial singularity of intimacy passage. Their individual relationship to life will be, on balance, reconciled, and their commitment to life service will be fully consecrated. These men will have the power to subdue their own demons and face down the embedded distortions of the culture's life-depleting paradigms. These will be men of integrity, and they will neither yield nor shrink away. They will not be distracted, bought off, exploited, manipulated, dismissed or otherwise compromised by power interests of the day. Neither will they indulge in the veneers of narcissism that so many bright lights of the past age have succumbed to. They will know an uncanny fidelity to their life cause, not compromising themselves to even a discreet degree. These actualized men will begin to represent coherent masculine activation to a culture and world ready for it in so many ways.

The effect these men will have on the masculine standard will be profound, impacting and influencing primarily women and young men. These two distinct groups are important because they will compel rapid change throughout the human condition, and the course of evolution will be expedited exponentially.

The example demonstrated by the emergence of actualized men who live by example their embodied clarity will inspire the idealism inherent in the general youthful male vigor. Young men can distinguish straw men from solid men as easily as women can. But young men cannot initiate themselves. However, through the examples of the new breed of masculine modeling, the cultures of the world will begin to respond with supportive social structures that embody the spirit of the new order of being, and young men will begin to receive a coherent nurturing from healthier culturing through their developmental years.

Women are critical to the process because their expectations and standards of men, if held to, will compel all men to respond to their influence. When the new order of actualized masculine expression emerges with enough men, women will begin to ground the criteria for male partnership in the possibilities demonstrated by these fully coherent men. This will effectively raise the bar for acceptable male expression. If the general cross section of heterosexual men want women in their lives they will be compelled to respond to the new standard.

The power to shift the current distorted male paradigm to this new vision and possibility should not be underestimated. This new class of extraordinary men will finally demonstrate the full masculine potentials of our time. They will redefine what is possible in male actualization not by preaching but by demonstrating a compelling living example. How they conduct themselves in the world of human affairs as artful and skillful men will begin to alchemize the evolutionary responsiveness existing within the current male psychic landscape. Young men and women will take notice as the tide begins to shift the zeitgeist around the general expectations of core male expression, marking the beginning of a new era of human unfolding. The grip of lost-male tyranny over the social structures we occupy will end, and subsequently release the hearts, minds and bodies of women and children the world over.

Iroquois: Feminine Integration of Social Structures

Integrating masculine archetypal action with the appropriate feminine archetypal complement in social structures is an unfulfilled art. The Iroquois Nation of the North American continent had succeeded to some degree at balancing the feminine process with the masculine dynamic within the culture, and the social structure reflected it. Iroquois family structures were all matrilineal. The women owned all property and they determined kinship. After marriage, a man moved into his wife's longhouse and their children became members of her clan. Marrying men into female matrilineal lines leveled the playing field and the balance of power within masculine/feminine relations by invoking the allegiance and service of the husband into his new family structure—that of his wife's heritage. By invoking a new husband's allegiance to and dependence on the wife's clan, the culture mitigated potentials for domestic violence and abuses of power by corrupt husbands. Alienating or mistreating an Iroquois wife meant you, as an offending husband, found yourself shunned, clanless and without a home.

The individual Iroquois tribes were divided into clans, each headed by the clan mother who, among other things, appointed male council members to act as representatives in tribal meetings. Iroquois chiefship titles were vested and appointed by the women who made up the matrilineal order of that clan. Instances of chief misconduct or incompetence resulted in replacement of that chief by the women who had placed him in that position of authority.

The dispersal of political authority to females having the power of appointing male leadership to office, combined with the vested power to remove and replace corrupt male chiefs, was a brilliant stroke of organizational savvy that reflected a clear understanding and respect for feminine integration to all aspects of social order. Subjecting masculine Iroquois rule to feminine oversight insured that male leaders would sublimate their ruling choices by honoring matriarchal considerations that by nature eschew totalitarianism.

Yet even this example of masculine and feminine archetypal balancing reflected in the old world social paradigm of the Iroquois must require evolution in the new era. The new movement toward evolution and wholeness through feminine integration will now be reflected in the men themselves, not just the crucible of the social construct they occupy and are beholden to. In the new order, men themselves will embody the refined features of a more balanced internal composite of archetypal polarity equilibrium. Expressing a more balanced integration of the masculine and feminine will allow men to relax with a full-form, core realization of their masculine potential and expression as men.

Dramatic outcomes of such change are not hard to imagine, but it is truly difficult to attempt to translate the nuanced shifts and transmutations that will occur on the heels of this kind of evolution, and the compelling and sublimely exquisite natures of them are myriad. It becomes an exercise in futility to distill in words a full apprehension of this vision while standing currently outside of the actualization of it all. I can say that we have only to venture into the intention of this possibility with a weighted conviction, and the realization of it will certainly be inevitable.

In Summary

In the final analysis, we are singular human beings in direct relationship with life. As men, indeed as human beings, we can never fully evolve until we penetrate deeper into our experience as purely living creatures and nothing more. What we will find at the end of that inquiry is a simple revelation. We will embrace the essential discovery that we are the created in relationship with the Creator. In a penultimate way we enjoy our diversity and similarities as human beings— black, white, boy, girl, picker, painter, professor, priest. But as men who humbly understand that we are first and foremost created creatures in primary connection to the Creator, we can ask the most liberating question: Is it so important that we as individuals personally survive, that we are willing to resort to contempt and violence as a cost to perpetuate our existence? If we as men were willing to live in such integrity that we would rather die than embrace a violent hypocrisy, then this world would look so incredibly different.

Every man who chooses integrity over self-interest changes the world with every authentic act he can manifest. If he manages to do that seamlessly from moment to moment, we witness a Christ or a Buddha, a being who shook the world. I propose that each of us is just a dormant world-shaker waiting to awaken. That is the promise of every true life-teacher who ever walked the earth.

A Final Thought for Men

Somewhere amid the self-absorbed swirl of dreamy half-men, the grace of our masculine fullness waits—absolutely still, with the patience of timelessness. That grace observes our forgetfulness but never abandons us.

Perhaps at times, we as men assault instead of caress because we imagine we really can somehow be separate creatures. It is an oversight that we really do perceive ourselves as fundamentally apart from life and one another. As men we miss so much, being rooted in this error.

How fast our minds must move to keep the truth of our glorious nature a blur. How hard our hearts must become to keep life's tenderness from being felt and received. How sophisticated our thinking must be so that the sublime simplicity of grace would appear unreasonable and foolish. We work so hard to build ramparts against the God that made us that we become exhausted and bitter from the effort.

And yet, our brief forms, like shadows, somehow sense the deeper sources from whence we came. Animating dust, infusing it with soul is the stuff of God, the very respiration of spirit in our corporal forms, and it is undeniably alive within us. We have only to perceive it. Nothing to gain. Nothing to lose. Nothing to control. It is all at hand, and has been since the beginning of time. We have only to claim it as our birthright.

A LETTER TO OUR GIRLS

It is difficult to find a dignified ground to stand upon while we as men try to express what it is we need to say to you after so many generations of recklessness in our treatment of you and the earth. There is a suffocating shame in our throats, awkward in the acceptance of our own actions. There is no excuse we can offer to offset the violence we have delivered. There is nothing but the raw hope of forgiveness, and perhaps an as yet unrealized dream of redemption.

Sweet sisters of ours, would you be willing to listen? We can only hope that perhaps there is yet left in your hearts an inclination to open to us again even some portion of that magnificently soft and radiant tenderness that we somehow forgot is what makes life worth living in the first place.

We promise in this moment, right now, to finally speak from our hearts and not our heads. So if you are willing to listen, we are appreciative and grateful for the opportunity.

Our fathers we understood to be good men for the most part. We needed to believe as boys that those men we called "Dad" knew more than we did about how life was to be lived. We looked to them for direction and guidance. As boys, we had little idea that our fathers, though perhaps well-intentioned, could be so misguided in so many ways. Yet such was our model, our blueprint to manhood. Like you as girls, we groped around at what our culture had to offer us as we grew into young adults. We see now that so much of the wisdom we needed as boys to be whole and beautiful men later in life was missing from our experience. And we also see now that so much of the information we did learn was startlingly flawed.

As men now, we make no excuse or justification for our errors. What is done cannot be undone. We see now that there is a power inside of us that we have used irresponsibly in the past, which we now commit to a radical correction, with an eye toward the redemption of our potential as authentic men in the world.

Our first act is toward our girls and toward the women to whom we owe everything. Without you we would be worse than totally empty, we would be agonizingly half empty. We can no longer bear to live with you suffering because of us. And so you are our first priority as we begin to repair the damage we have done.

Because we acknowledge that we need you to accomplish anything that we attempt to do in the world, we ask for your blessing and your help. You will continue to remain our first priority from this time forward. This we promise as men to do. And this we promise as men to teach our boys, now and for always.

Your feminine radiance we promise to nurture and delight in. Your tenderness and vulnerability we promise to protect. Your wisdom we promise to bow before, and your heart we promise to serve. Your wild, unqualified and untamed nature we commit to humble ourselves before. In every act of every day, not one portion of these oaths to you will be broken, and our duty toward you as husbands, fathers, brothers and sons will be uncompromised.

We will attempt to bear the brunt of the suffering that life may offer up before it reaches you, and like a tall fence encircling a beautiful garden, we will position ourselves to protect and insulate that which is most precious to us from harm. For all these acts we thank you for the opportunity that you give us in living a fulfilling life of service to beauty and truth, saving us from the petty personal ambitions that drove our fathers and continue to drive broken and hollow men today.

We have been lost. We have caused great damage. But through grace we are delivered now into the heart of our true nature, and we devote and dedicate our masculine core to the noble husbandry we were born to practice.

We as committed men ask only one thing of you. We wish that in order to help all men heal without exception, you choose only those men who are consecrated to this sacred endeavor. We ask that you keep your precious temples unavailable to any of our lost brothers who may seek your bodies and your radiance. We pray that you deliver your hearts only to the proven authentic masculine suitor. You are the most powerful influence in our lives. What you require of us as men will in time cause us to respond to your birthright as women. Please insist of us what beauty and integrity we are capable of. Please demand of us the type of man you are so worthy of. We humbly ask your patience as we find our way on this new journey, yet we desire that you refrain from compromise. May we draw inspiration and wisdom from your example of grace and strength.

We promise to be responsible to you as women as you relinquish the masculine burden you have taken on in your lives. We want you to be the radiant feminine you were designed to be, and to finally be able to relieve yourself of the drain of having to compensate for the betrayal of our forefathers. We, the living men of this age, vow right now to end the unnecessary suffering you have for so long endured. It is the least we can do.

You have heard reconciliatory words before, endured empty promises whose sentiment seemed on target. We know that it may be hard to believe that as men we could actually do this. But the time is at hand, and we know your exquisite intuitive capacities can feel the truth of this.

We will take the first step, but we will soon need your willingness to believe that we can be the men you are so worthy of having in your lives. So why not expect it? For if one man can feel it in his heart enough to write this and can be committed enough to actualize it in his life as a matter of course, then the testimony is already made, the vision has begun to unfold.

You are one sister reading this. I am one brother writing it. The fire is already started...

EPILOGUE

When come soft rains on window panes
And autumn winds are blown.

When tranquil times invoke my rhymes
And the seeds of heart are sown.

— From *When Come Soft Rains*

Subjective Positioning

Writing a book (or crafting any art for that matter) can pigeonhole you if you aren't careful. As soon as you lay the words down, somebody has you evaluated and labeled. It just comes with the territory of people saying what they think when you express a position.

Conceptual positions are interesting things. When we hold to a particular viewpoint or value judgment or retain a certain sense of what appears to be true to us, we operate out of that premise. We position ourselves to be loved or despised by those who review where we stand.

My values and perceptions come out of a lifetime of feeling into my heart and trusting the voice that is there, and while some of the perceptions expressed here may carry a congruency with religious and/or moralistic positions, the derivation and nature of those positions could not be more different.

I am neither threatened nor put off by the fact that others may not share my particular perceptions. The fact that my values are not belief-based means that I do not require a group or community to provide any sort of affirmation to sustain those current values.

And my perceptions change, as I have experienced my whole life. To hold to static ideology, however profound, is to engage in a death grip with life itself. For what is relevant now may be defunct tomorrow. Besides, every stroke of brilliance is at best a temporary road sign and nothing more.

Life is movement and change, with some sense of relative patterning within a matrix of quantum flux. To stiffen up and hold on to old concepts for fear of new understandings is a recipe for suffering.

Caveat Emptor

The subject of coherent masculine integration is a very comprehensive matter. In *Razing Men*, I wanted to accomplish a meaningful overview of the subject, so I opted to cover more ground with less extensive exposition. There are perhaps a hundred other books that could spring out of the material grist of *Razing Men*. My hope is that this book serves as a solid foundation toward a beginning or further exploration of the subject of coherent core masculine integration and expression.

On that journey, it is inevitable that authentic inquiry is going to challenge the existing cultural paradigms that are currently influencing us as men. Confronting the many contours and layers of corruption and distortion in our culture is essential, though the scope of it is broad and deep. However, any thoroughly legitimate approach to core masculine reformation must leave no stone unturned.

Cultures by nature shun certain change, and power paradigms abhor most any form of it. Leveling the existing flawed paradigms and sacred cows of the day will not leave much standing in the aftermath; so it is. I have not come to this call necessarily to make political allies. I am interested in what is true, plain and simple. If I find something that brings us as living creatures closer to coherency, I will give testimony to it. So if you embark on this journey as men, take heart, and be bold.

To this end, I admire Union General William Tecumseh Sherman. He accepted probably more than most in his time that there was nothing civilized or restrained about war, and as a soldier he was not afraid to conduct his duty straight through the ugliness of it without apology. An honest man of action is hard to find, and if you don't know enough of them, then maybe become one yourself—the world could use you.

Where I'm Coming From

After building an off-the-grid, rammed-earth, self-sustaining, passive and active solar home in the Rocky Mountains in the summer of 1999, many people asked me if I was an architect, or an engineer.

"No," I would invariably say, "But I studied a few before I built it."

Likewise, a lot of people have asked me during the writing of this book, "Are you a philosopher? A warrior? Transpersonal psychologist? Mythologist? Divinity teacher? Lawyer? Sociologist? Cultural anthropologist? Minister? Spiritual teacher? Shaman? Psychotherapist? Social worker? Politician? Mystic? Medicine man?

"No," I would invariably say, "But I studied a few before I wrote it."

I'm a big fan of self-education. Most of what I know I didn't learn in the few odd years I spent in college. Whatever I have a passion for I learn about in my own way. I absorb from those whom I feel are masters in a certain field or craft. Then I fold it all into my own intuition and insight. The result is the tonal authority with which I move and express myself in the world. I put a lot of stock in that brand of understanding and action. It doesn't always mean I'm right, but it does mean that what comes through me is valid, even if it's not sanctified by the traditional reviewers and teachers of existing social paradigms.

Scholars who write books within their field of study tend to move in ways that bind them to the scope of their traditional learning. It's a limitation I am happy to be free of. I move into a subject with a broad stroke, and I am open to possibilities that may fly in the face of accepted interpretations. I don't worry much about the consequences or the academic scrutiny that comes from standing on new or unconventional ground. I am interested in the truth of the matter and nothing more.

I have never intended this book to be a scholarly treatise. I would be happy if it were closer in practicality to a crescent wrench, accessible to every man, be he artist, student, laborer or scholar. For me, *Razing Men* needed to express something that had not quite been said yet, or certainly not in this way before.

One thing I know, whatever feels accurate and alive about *Razing Men* was already known to the reader to be true long before I ever wrote it. In the end, this book is just a static reference tool, and it is you, the reader, who possesses the living instrument that gives testimony and actualization to anything in it that feels true.

A Fan of Man

Some readers might think I've been a little hard on the male gender—that perhaps I put too much responsibility upon one gender for the ills of the human condition. Fair enough. Maybe I have. But only because I am myself a man and only because I see so much unrealized potential in our gender.

A beautiful man is equally as magnificent as a beautiful woman. I love a real man, am proud to call him my brother, proud to work and play and fight by his side. But men not seated in their authentic masculine core have always been peculiar creatures to me. Whether they are actively violent or passively contributing to the violence by doing nothing about it has for me all added up to the same display of unnecessary error.

At work, at play, on the field of competition, in fistfights and in leisure moments, I have engaged my fellow brothers time and time again, and I have known more beauty than error, and I know that the flaws that exist in between are neither irredeemable nor inherent. Men want excellence of expression as much as women want to feel a connectivity to it through them.

We are brothers one and all, with so many different names. Muslim, Christian, Buddhist, Hindu, agnostic, gay, straight, Chinese, Swedish and a million other designations. Diversity is beautiful, but we must not forget that one step removed from our ethnic and cultural differences is our fundamental unity, and we must know the latter before we can fully celebrate the former.

I trust that men are not violent by nature. They are lovers. My dad always used to say in defense of men, "Who has written most all of the romantic love songs?" He was right. Men just need to understand the truth of their birthright as clear masculine agents in the world and move beyond all this confusion and distortion into the huge hearts they were born to occupy.

And so the last words in this book I borrow from my father and give to you:

"Here's to love and understanding, and may wisdom and intelligence flourish and become the fertile ground where seeds of both may blossom and grow, and embrace us, and all mankind."

ACKNOWLEDGEMENTS

I would like to thank a few lights who influenced my soul in ways that I can still feel today.

Thanks to my brother, Chuck Revel, who demonstrated the power and ferocity of the protective masculine while standing up for his little brother countless times in the midst of much chaos growing up. His presence was in many ways the best place I knew of in my childhood.

Thanks to my father, Frank Revel, who passed on while I was writing this book. We understood things in ways that made for a rapport between us that I miss deeply. He gave me his pain around the misfires in the human condition. His mind was sensitive, brilliant, witty and clever. He taught me to dream big and have the audacity to think I could make it real. I still hear him saying "atta boy!"

Thanks to my mother, Dolores, who loves her son the way only mothers can, the way that makes a man feel like someone on this planet will stand by him, no matter what the hell he does or how badly he screws up. Ask any man how much that means to him. It has meant everything to me.

Thanks to my 5th-grade basketball coach, Chris Camalari, who may not know it but was the first adult male I ever interacted with at length who was consistently safe and benevolent. He showed me the beauty of masculine tenderness and recognized the light and power in my youthful heart.

Thanks to my sister, Connie Abbott, for making me realize, at a very young age, that I had a knack for the written word. Thanks to my brother-in-law, Bob Abbott, for being a masculine rock whom I could always consider in my youth as a good and decent man.

Thanks to my first life mentor, Alice Simms, a then-76-year-old woman whom I met while delivering flowers as a 16-year-old boy. I studied with her every week for over a decade. She patiently introduced me to all the great lights of human history and changed the course of a young man's life forever. My time with her, and the profound effect it had on my life, is itself a whole other book as yet unwritten. I miss the fire in her eyes and the passion in her soul.

Thanks to my ex-wives, Valerie and Marcee, who remain dear friends today. They accompanied an unripe man through some portion of his life with grace and genuine love. Valerie was the perfect fit for me in those very early days and we had a great run together. Marcee is an amazing soul who delights in the journey to full awareness, and my marriage to her was an adventure that was incredibly healing to my tattered soul. I am lucky to have journeyed together with these beautiful women.

Thanks to Thom Garcia, my best male friend in the world, and my favorite all-time dude. I have faith in this guy in every way you can believe in someone, a fellow of total integrity. If I were President, he would be my most trusted advisor. A straight-up, no-BS man who is funny as hell. Lucky is the woman who gains his affections, and blessed am I for having him as a best friend all these years.

Thanks to the many men I communed with in H-unit at San Quentin State Prison. There, in what was the last place I would have guessed, I found hope for the redemption of the masculine heart. Inside those concrete-and-steel walls I found the hearts of men that time forgot—but *I* will never forget. The power of their gift to me, in many ways, has delivered this book to you.

Thanks to Dr. Marshall Rosenberg, the man who turned my world around with his brilliant work of language models that demonstrates heartfelt communication. Marshall became for me, when I studied with him, my adopted paternal icon. He showed a confused young man (me) something every father should reveal to his son: the power of heart over head and the beauty of an open hand rather than a fist. And God bless him, because he understood both intimately.

Thanks to Adyashanti, though I always told him jokingly that his adopted "spiritual" name almost stopped me from going to see him initially. God help me, I had endured too many holy names and not enough content in my early seeking days. But who cares about names when you find a brother like him on the path. This regular American guy has managed to find a seamless liberation into the full expression of humanness. He is the most exquisite embodiment of coherent male core realization I have ever come across. His was for me an instruction by transmission and not just a teaching of inspired words. Thank God for Adyashanti, a truly realized teacher I could also play Frisbee with.

Thanks to the amazing Catharine Merkel who boldly decided to let me into her abundant heart. That she chose to receive me so fully reveals volumes about her graceful power and beauty. To me she has the effect the feminine ought to have on a man. I can pay no woman a deeper compliment. Her influence is everywhere in this book, just as it is in every other action I take in the world while we are coupled. To my beloved Cathie, the talented goldsmith, not only do you have way cooler hand tools than me, but you have made the possibility of experiencing the alchemy of an unalloyed love a reality, and made the pages on romantic partnership in this book not just words, but a living testimony.

Thanks to Ruby and Roxanne, Catharine's beautiful daughters. Though I am not the lucky man who gets to be called your biological father, you have let me into your hearts and worlds so that I may roar like a lion standing over his pride. What you girls have done for my heart and soul is immeasurable. I delight in you both as young ladies, adore your individual hearts and just plain love you girls something fierce. I will have had a full life if I manage to do little else than con-tribute some consistent measure of good service to your precious lives.

Thanks to my editor, Rose Marie Cleese, whom I actually hope to meet one day in person! Her eagle eye and spot-on treatment of this material has turned a hairy beast of a manuscript into a well-groomed book you might actually invite to tea. Thanks to your unearthly knowledge of the English language and your authoritative command over the written word, I sit, stand and lie down corrected—that being a good thing. Thank you for a lightning-fast job that was thorough and totally attuned to my vision.

Thanks to Caren Parnes, the rock upon whom I am able to publish this book. When I told her my dream of holding *Razing Men*, the book, in my hands by July of 2011, she made it happen. If any aspiring writers out there embark upon the adventure of self-publishing, I pray you ei-ther have Caren, or someone her equivalent (if that's possible), on board. Much gratitude to you, Caren.

And finally, thanks to you, the reader. I may not yet, or ever, know you, but one thing I do know: the content of this book can only be sanctioned by the heart of the reader. Thank you for giving it your attention, and by all means pass it on if it resonated with your soul.

About the Author

Author, teacher, visionary and founder of GO Divorce Clinic, **Robert Revel** has been a passionate life student of the art of moving awareness through the instrument of the human body. That journey began in earnest for Robert at the age of 16 when he began a serendipitous 12-year apprenticeship with Alice Simms, a consciousness teacher 60 years his senior. Alice exposed him to the works and spiritual teachings of some of the world's most luminous minds—from Rumi to Paramahansa Yogananda.

After studying film production in college and a brief stint in the commercial film industry, Robert became a trainer with Dr. Marshall Rosenberg's Center for Nonviolent Communication in 2001. He began a journey teaching the art of transforming violence everywhere he could: in prisons, schools, intentional communities, homeless shelters and with spiritual groups. Following this, he began a period of extensive travel, searching and studying with consciousness teachers from diverse cultures around the world. Returning home, he began integrating a personal study of systems theory, quantum awareness fields and organizational dynamics. This enrichment enabled him to expand his reach to corporate administrators, athletic teams, juvenile offender programs and, through the court system, divorcing families—a demographic he focuses on today. He holds a Mediation Certificate from John F. Kennedy University and a Paralegal Certificate from the University of California at Santa Cruz, and he is a Certified Practitioner of the dimensionally healing art of Jin Shin Jyutsu.

A prolifically creative man, Robert has written and directed six independent films; published poetry, screenplays, magazine articles and newspaper columns; and composes music as a hobby. He designed and built his own rammed-earth, off-the-grid home in the Rocky Mountains, where he lived a self-sustaining lifestyle for eight years. Recently, he founded the innovative GO Divorce Clinic in Sonoma County, California, which focuses on a humanized, attorney-free divorce model he envisioned, a divorce process that makes what is typically an overwhelming experience affordable and accessible to many. He lives in the beautiful wine country town of Healdsburg with his dog, Sneffles.

For more information on Robert Revel or to contact the author, you may visit www.robertrevel.com.

CPSIA information can be obtained
at www.ICGtesting.com
Printed in the USA
LVOW04s1345071016
507850LV00016B/425/P